**MRR Coloring Pages**

# 150 Mesmerizing Coloring Pages
# Beautiful Butterflies

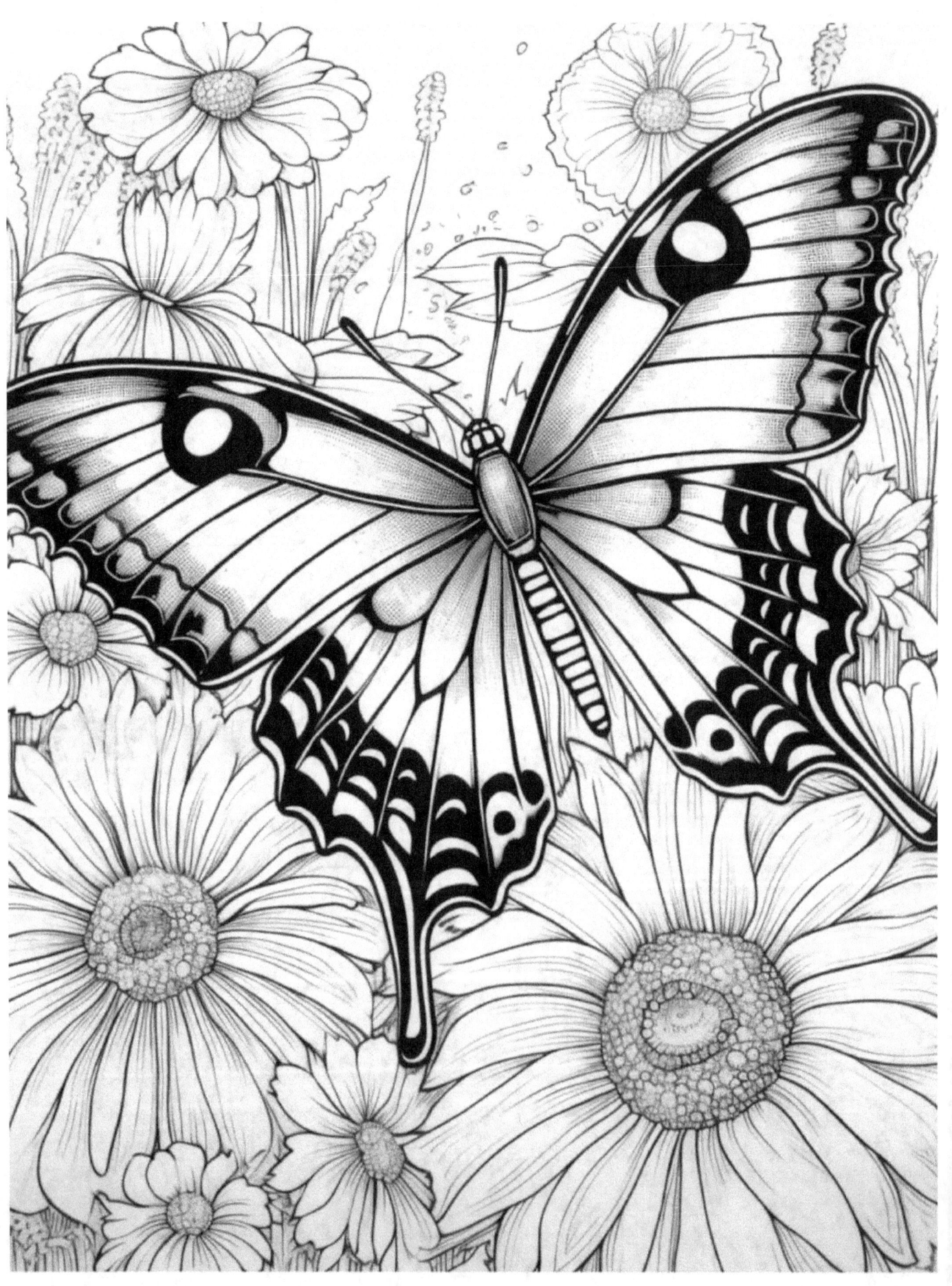

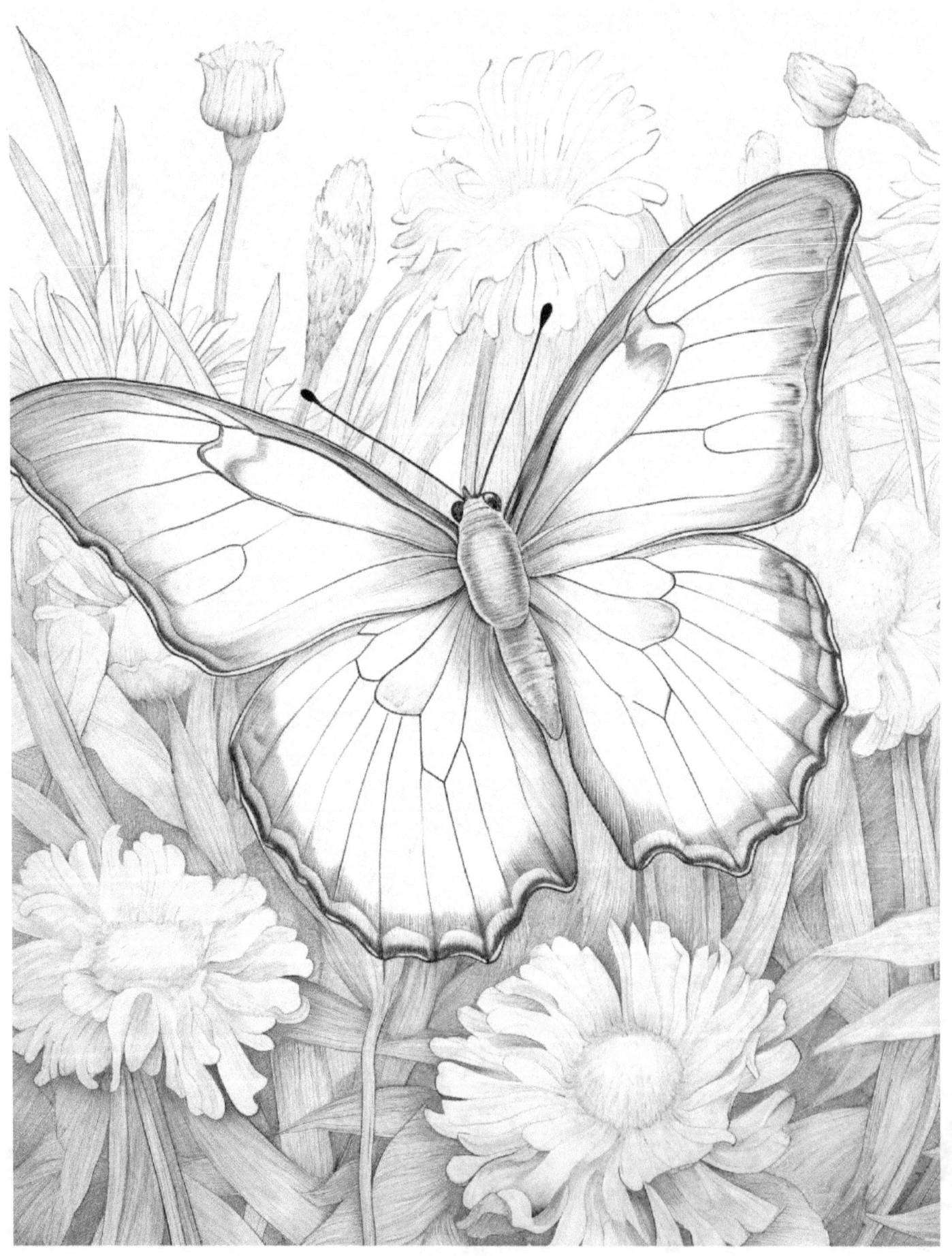

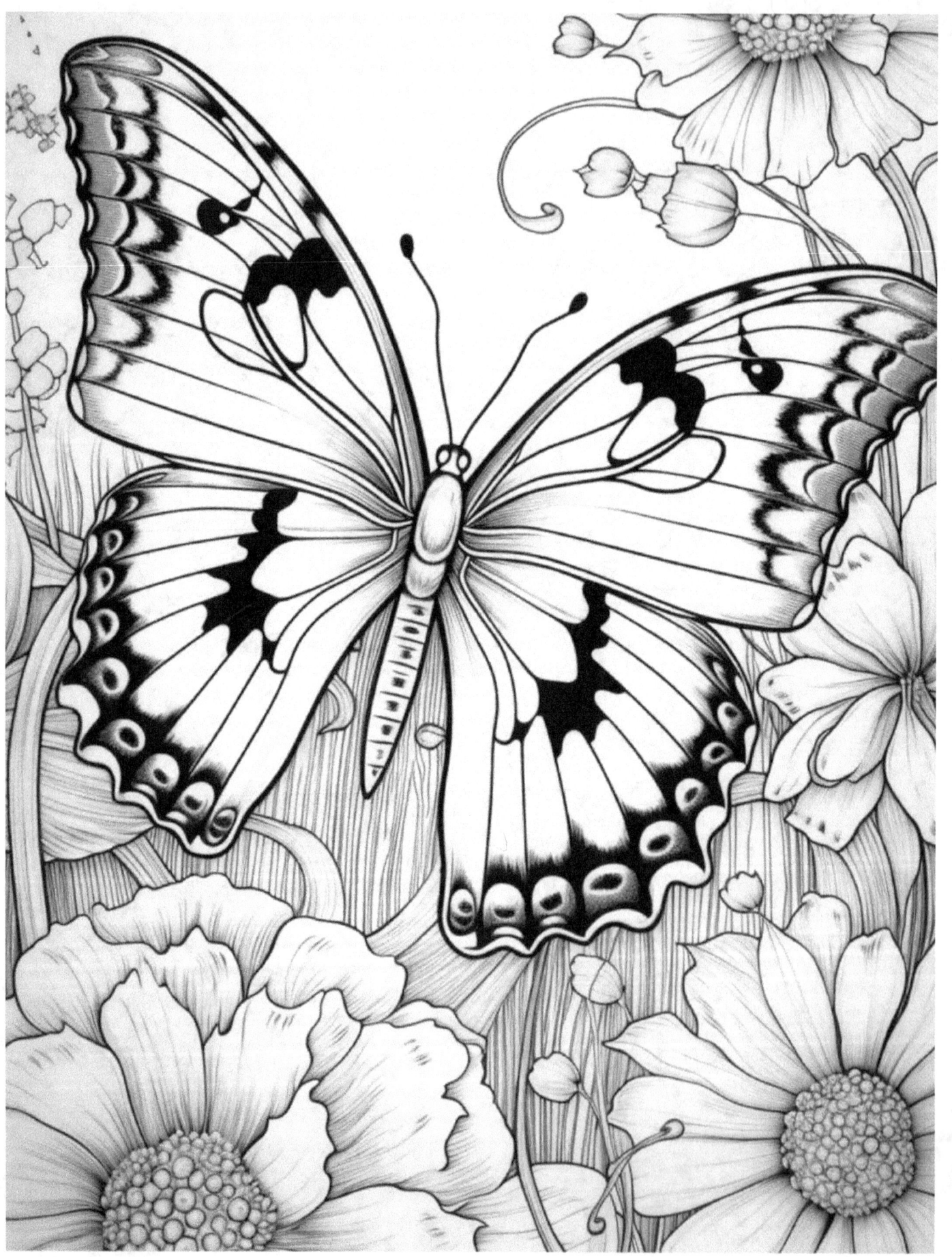

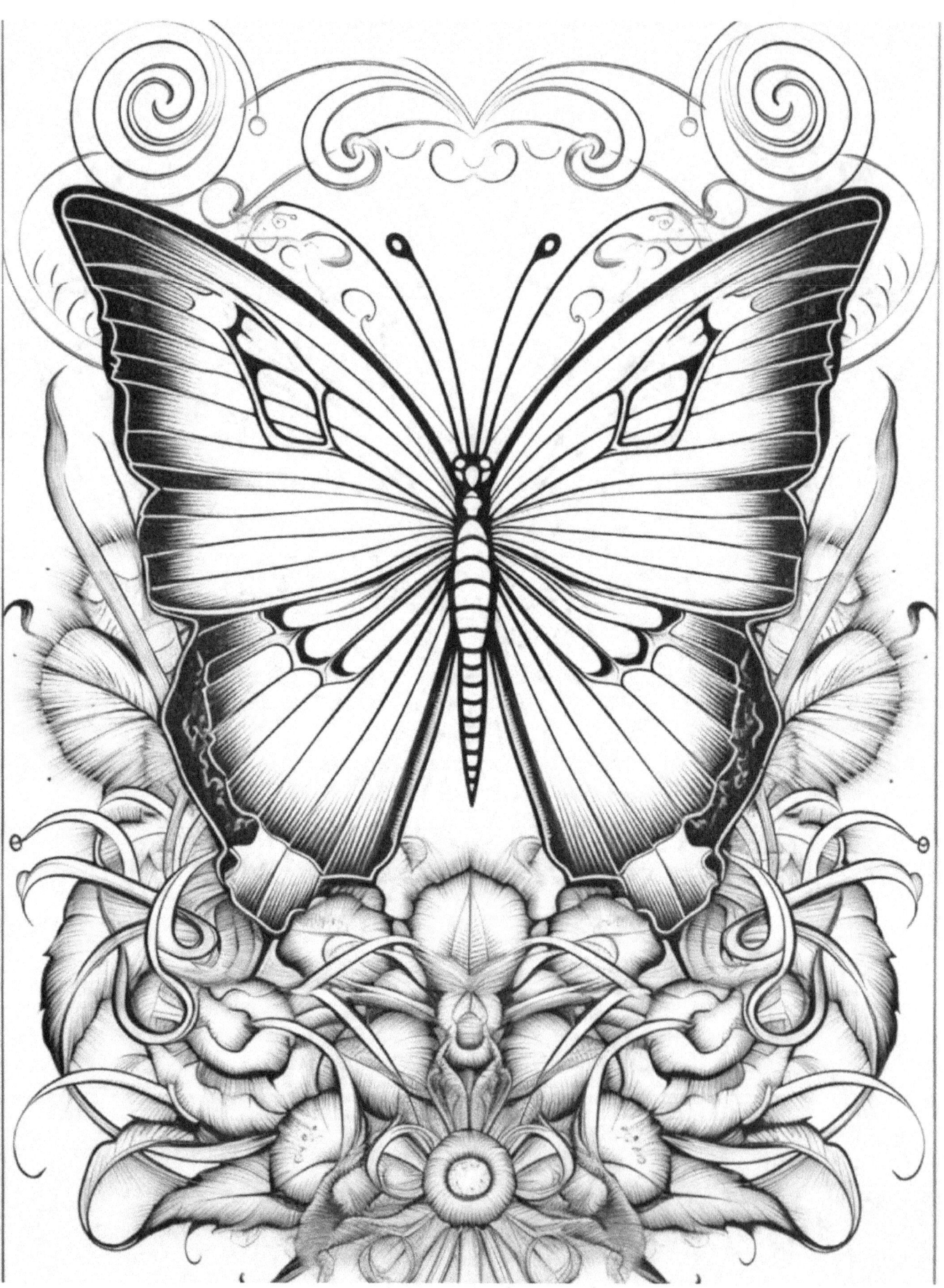

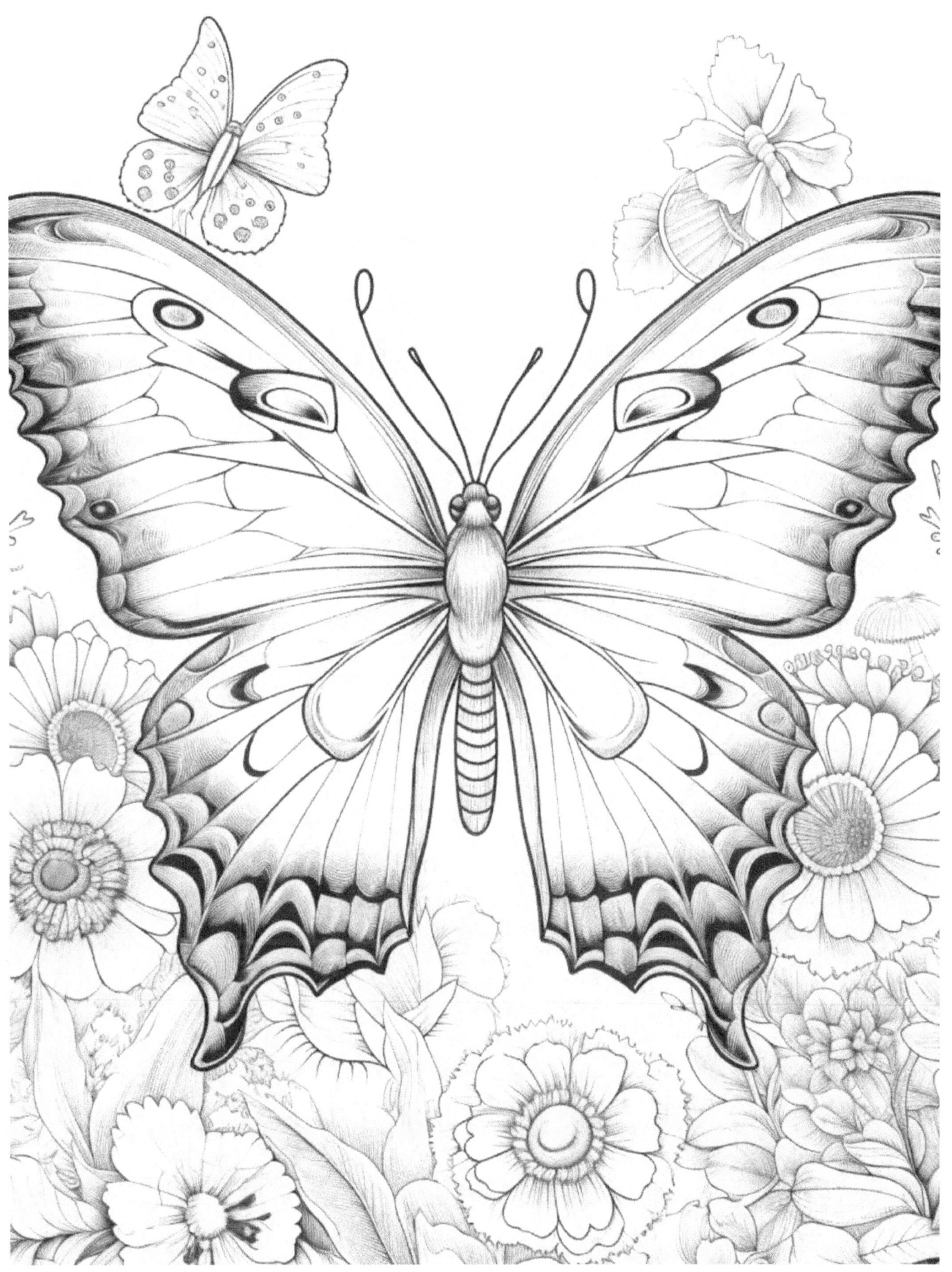

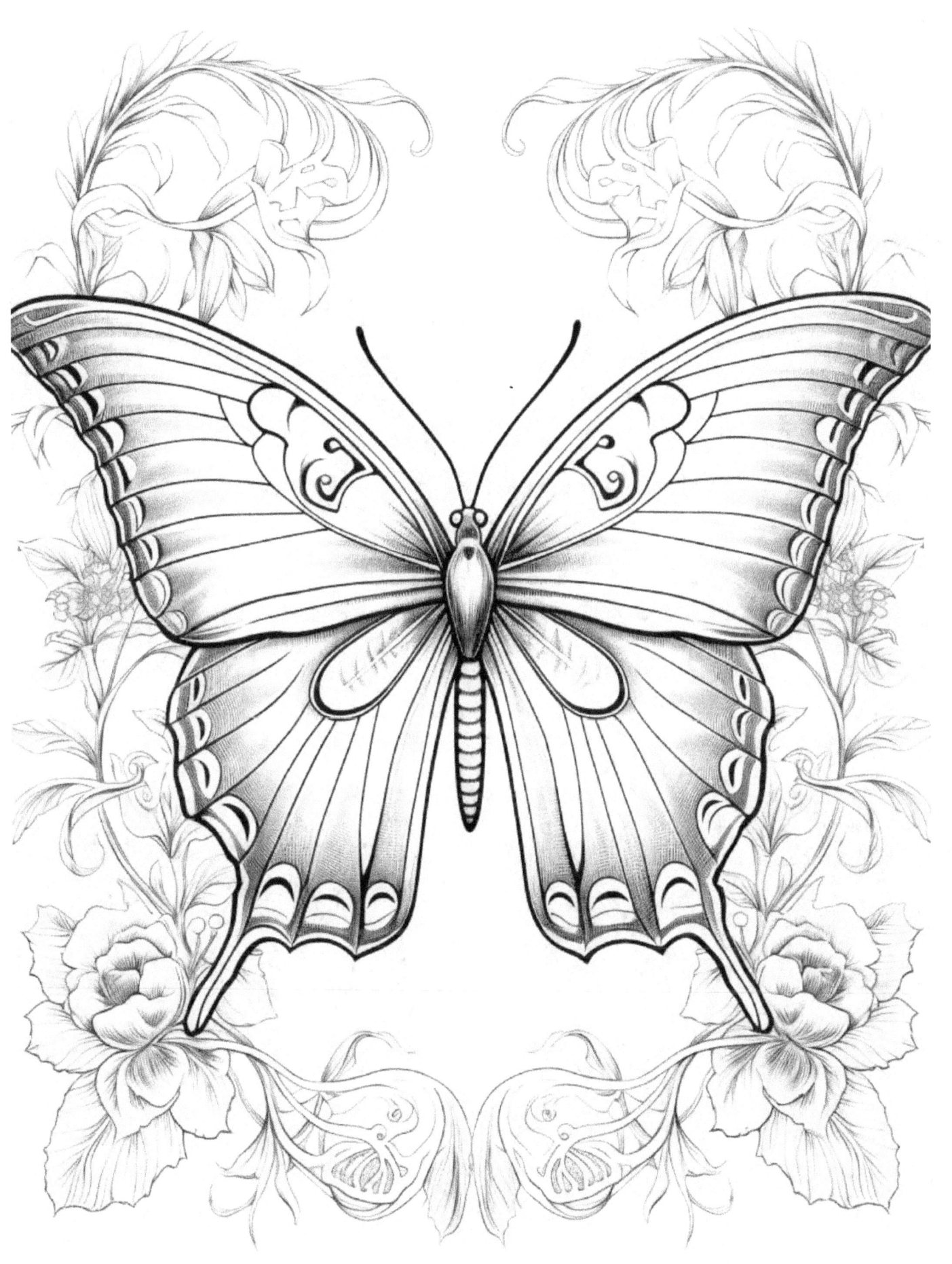

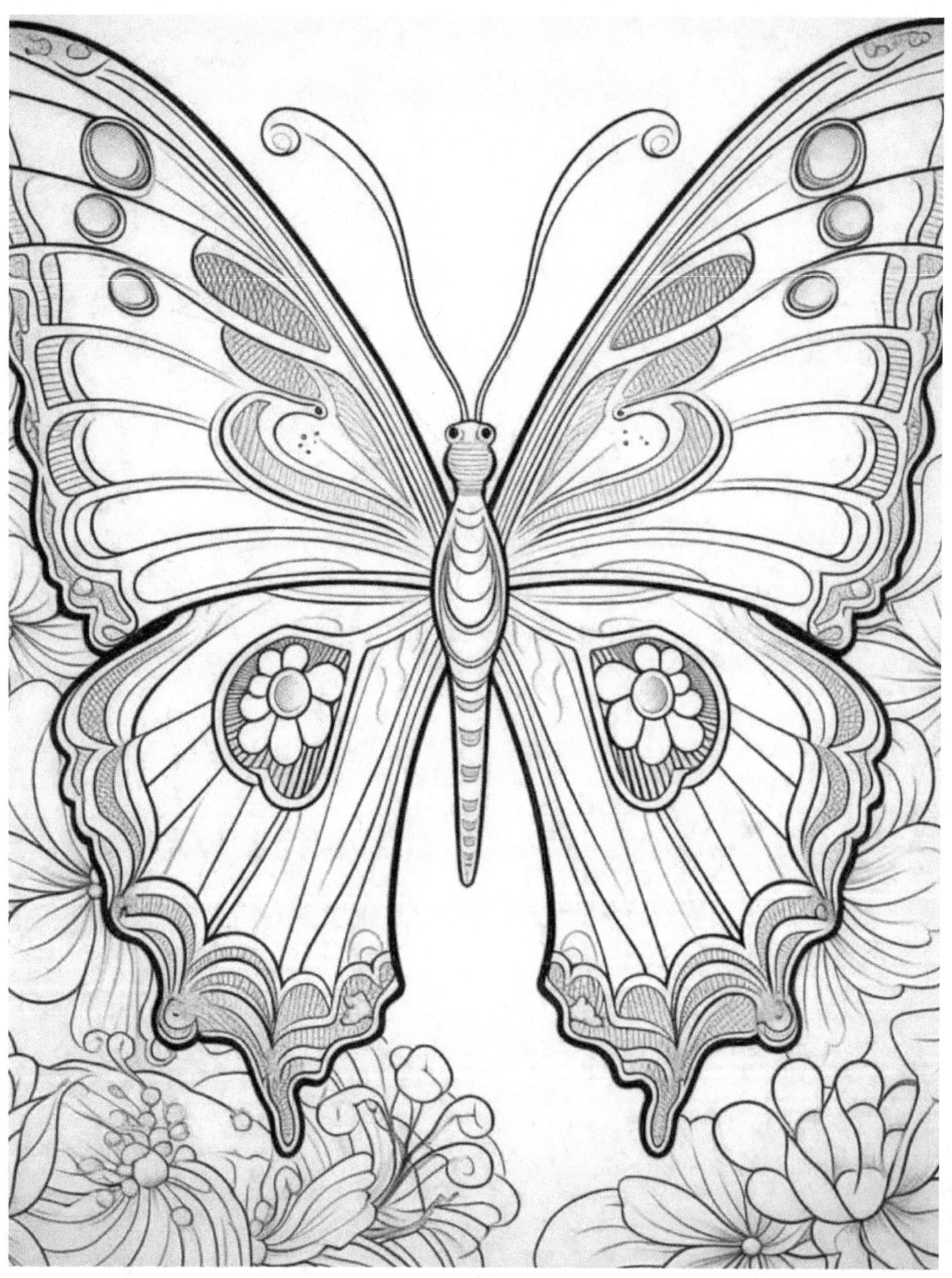

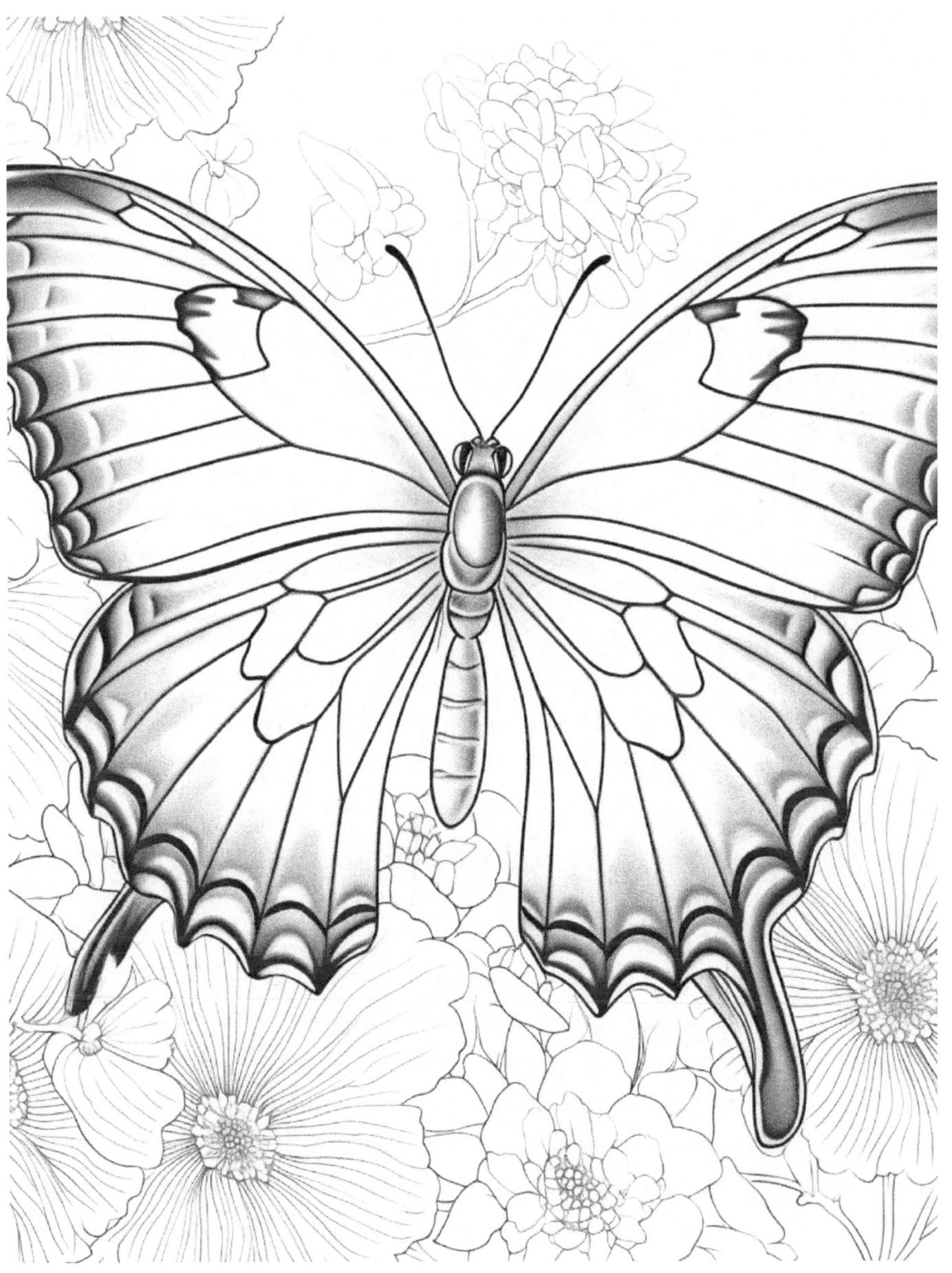

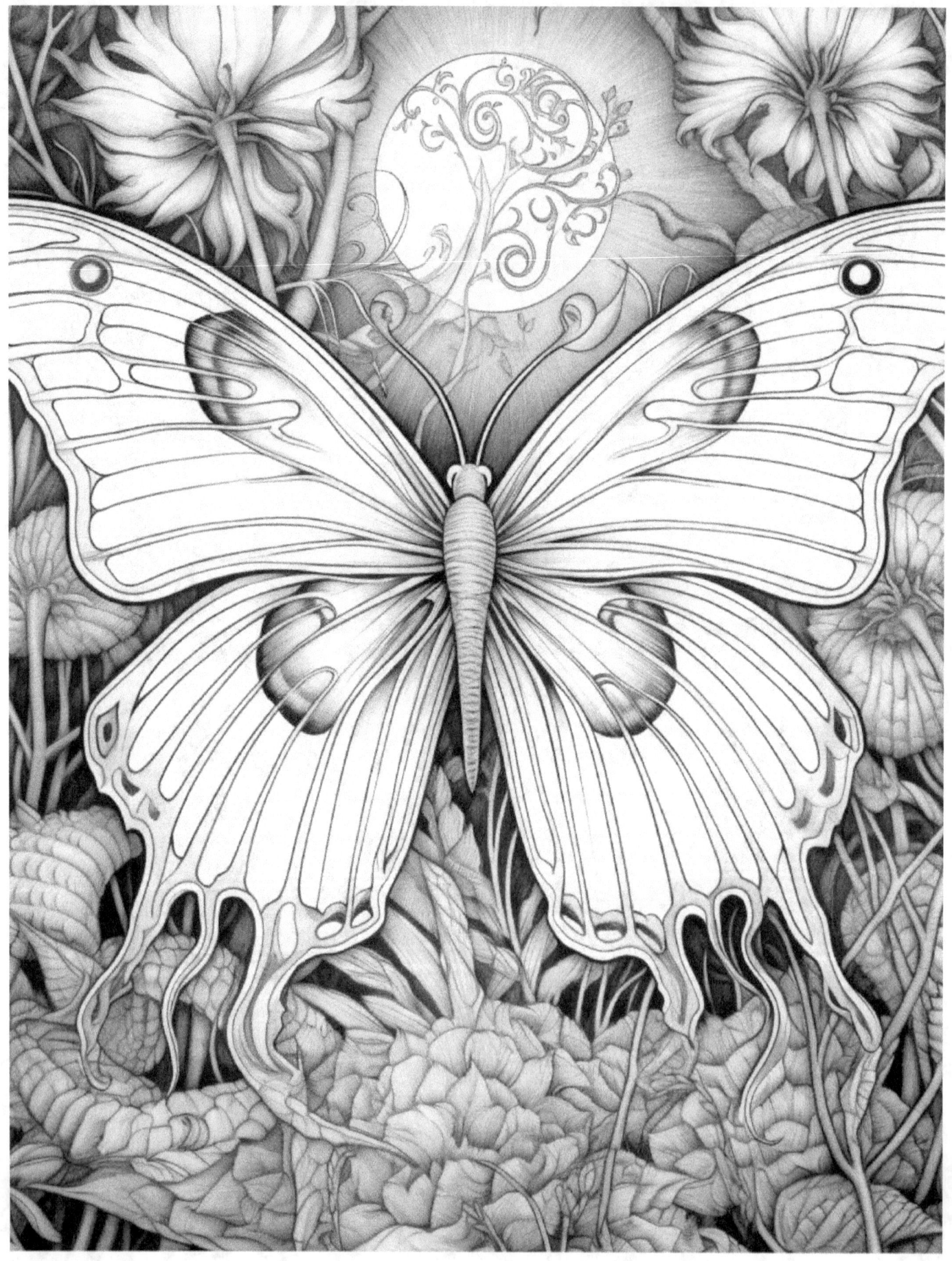

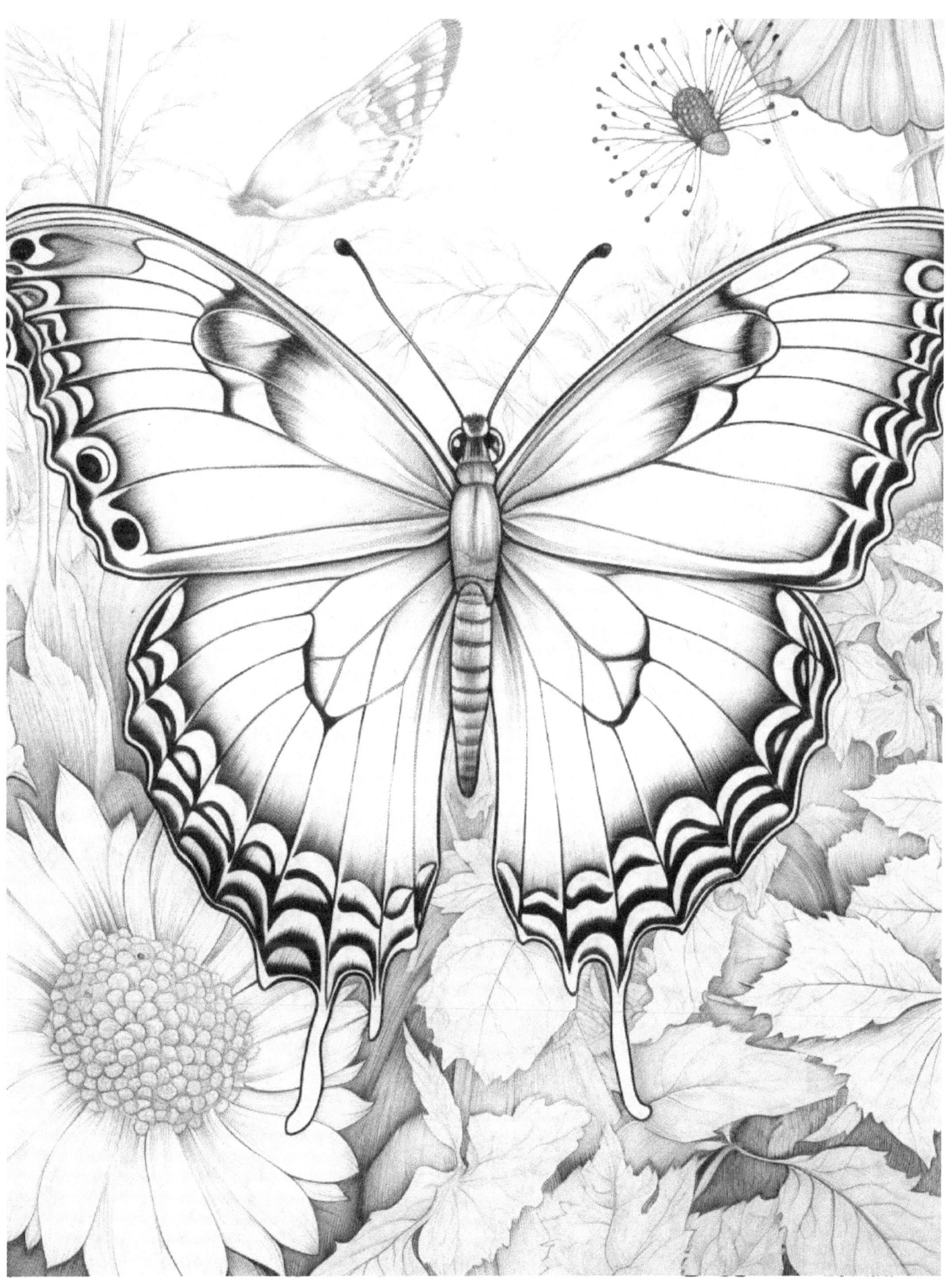

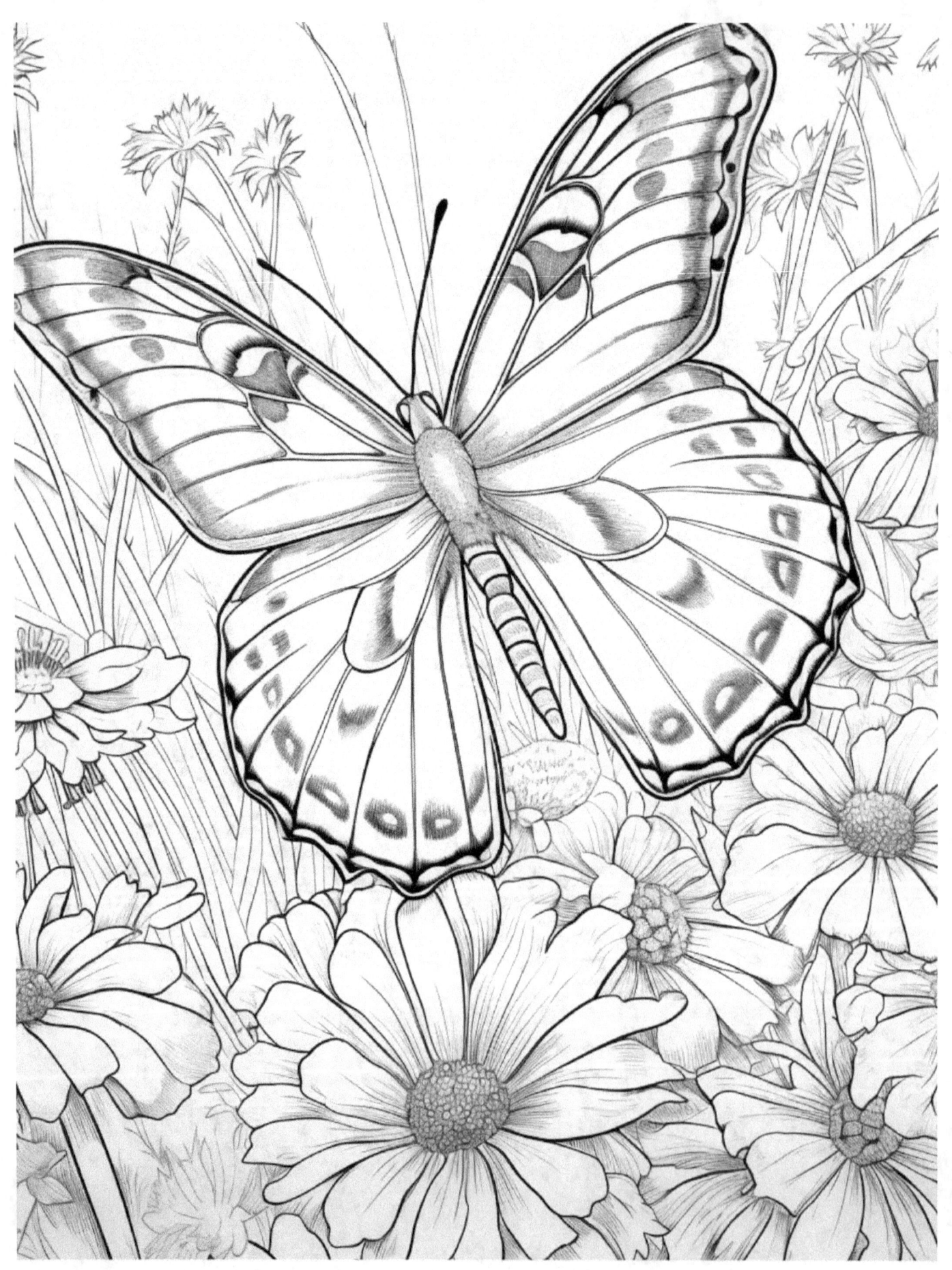

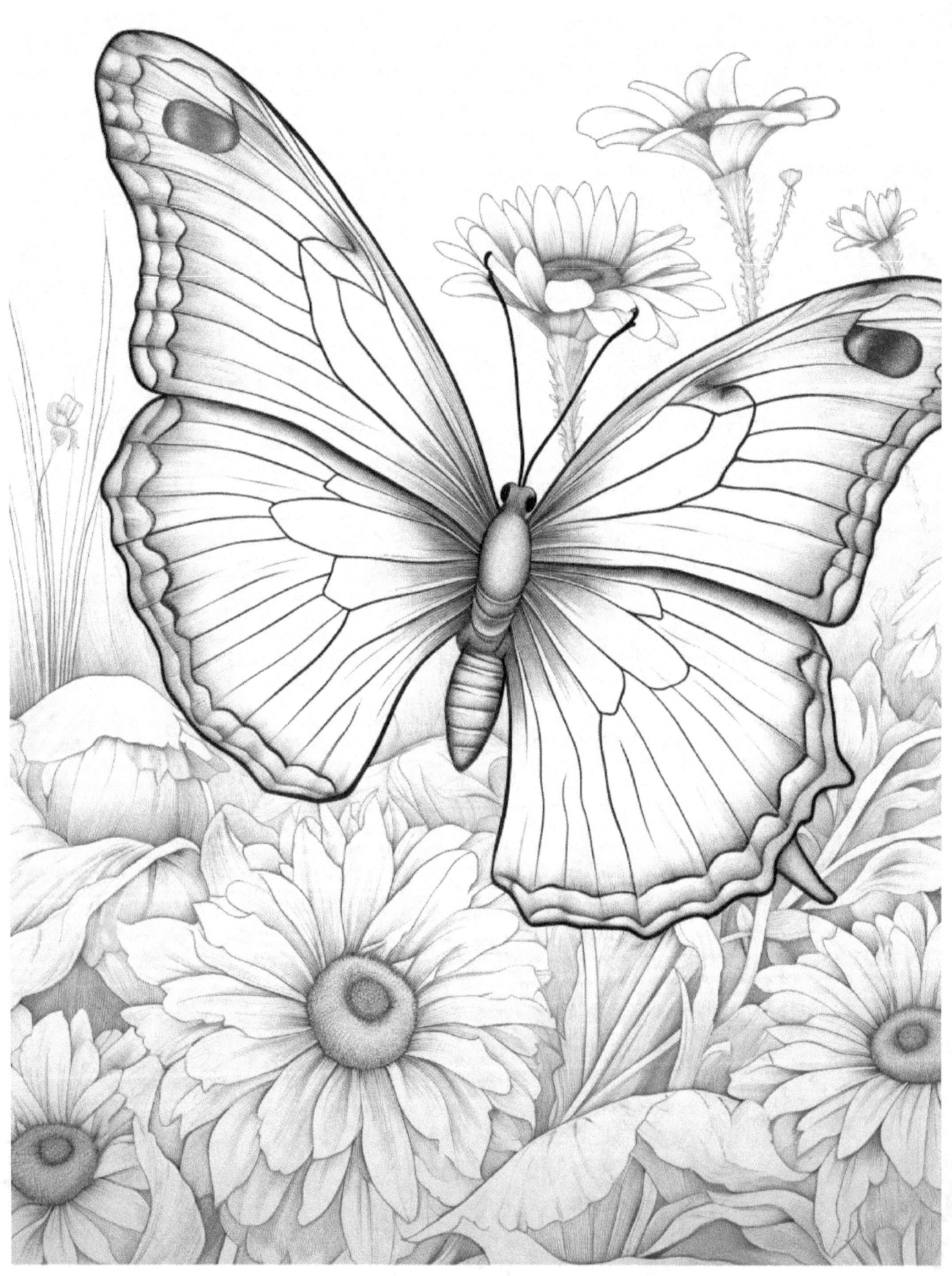

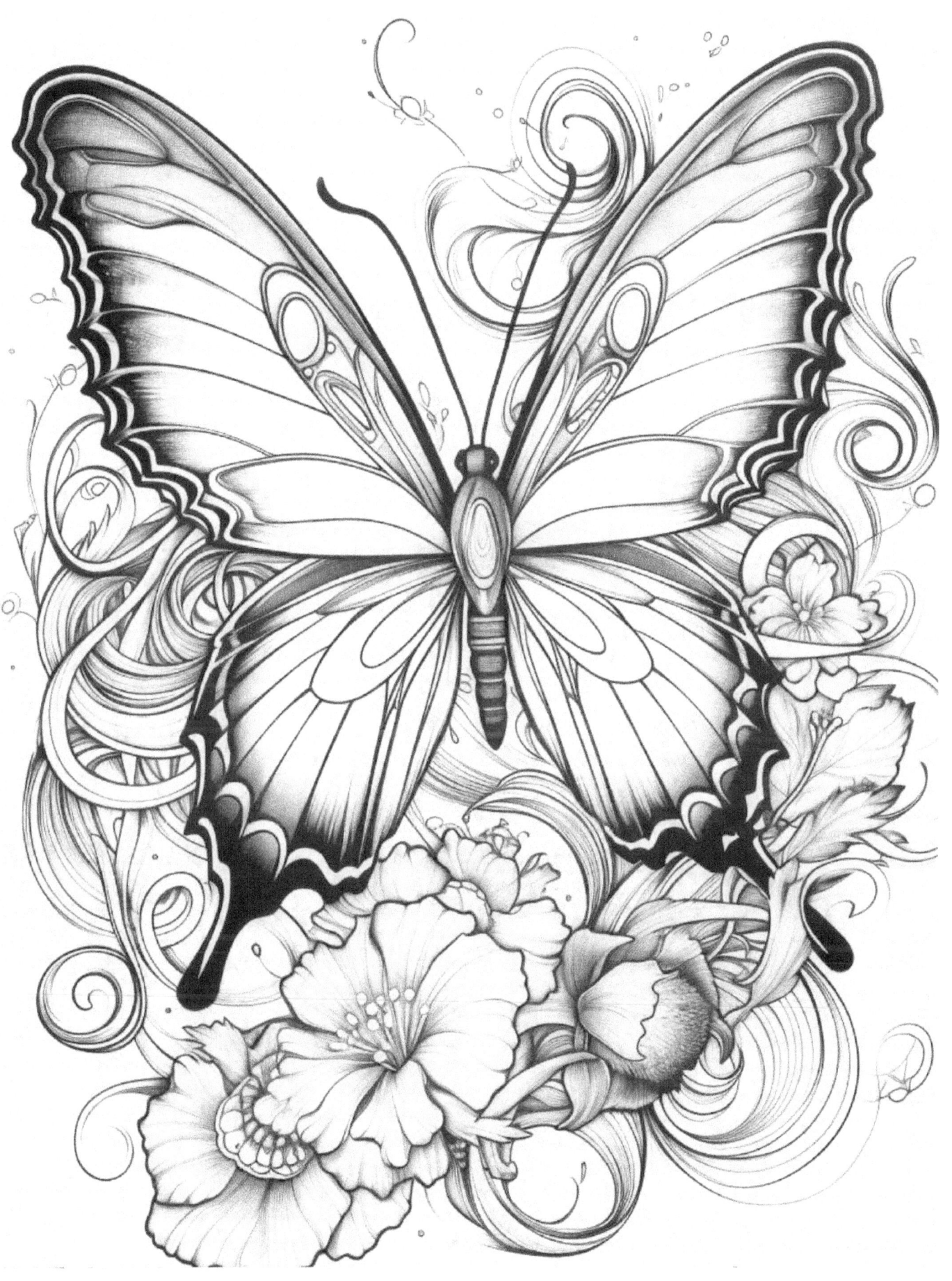

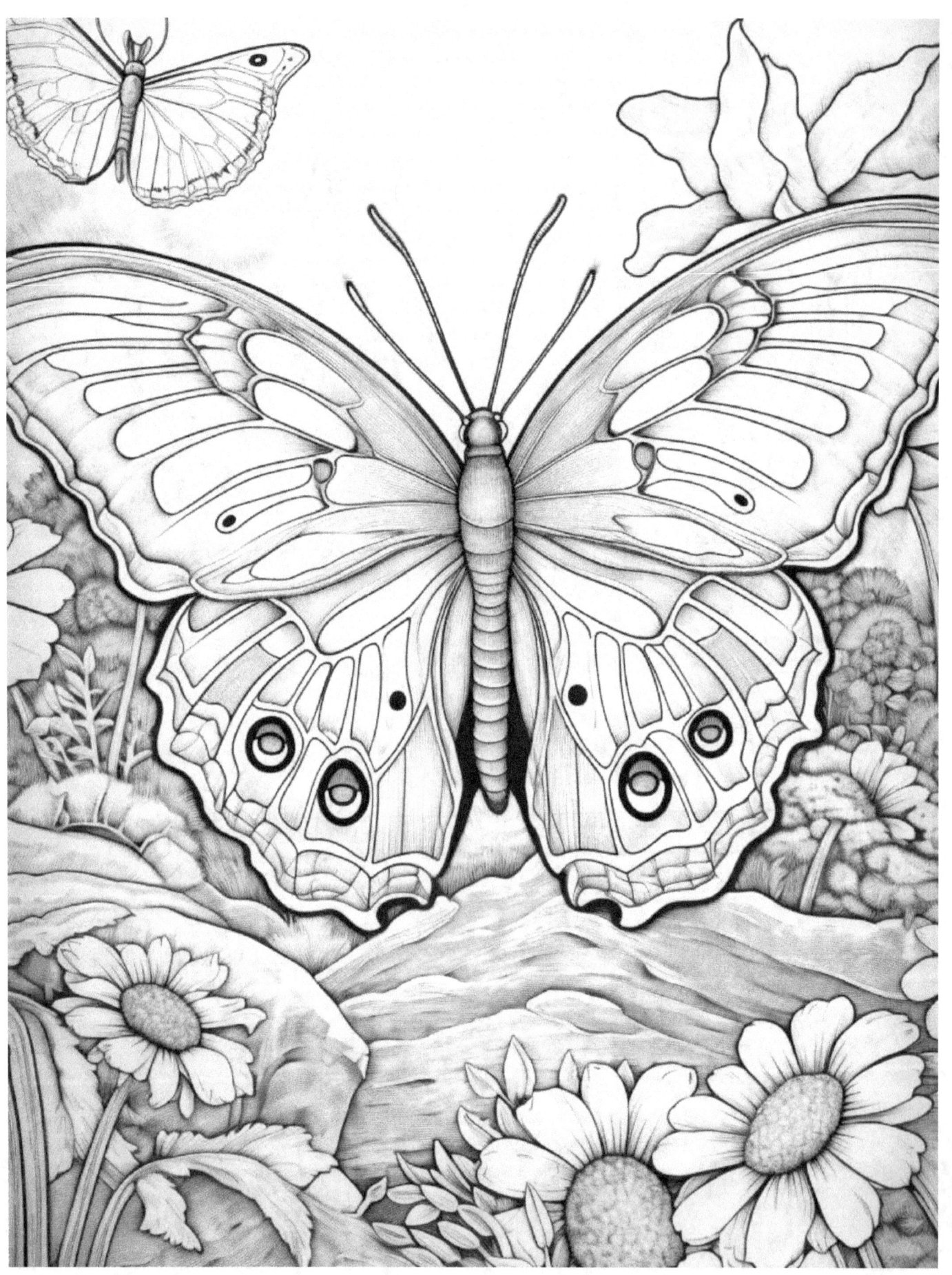

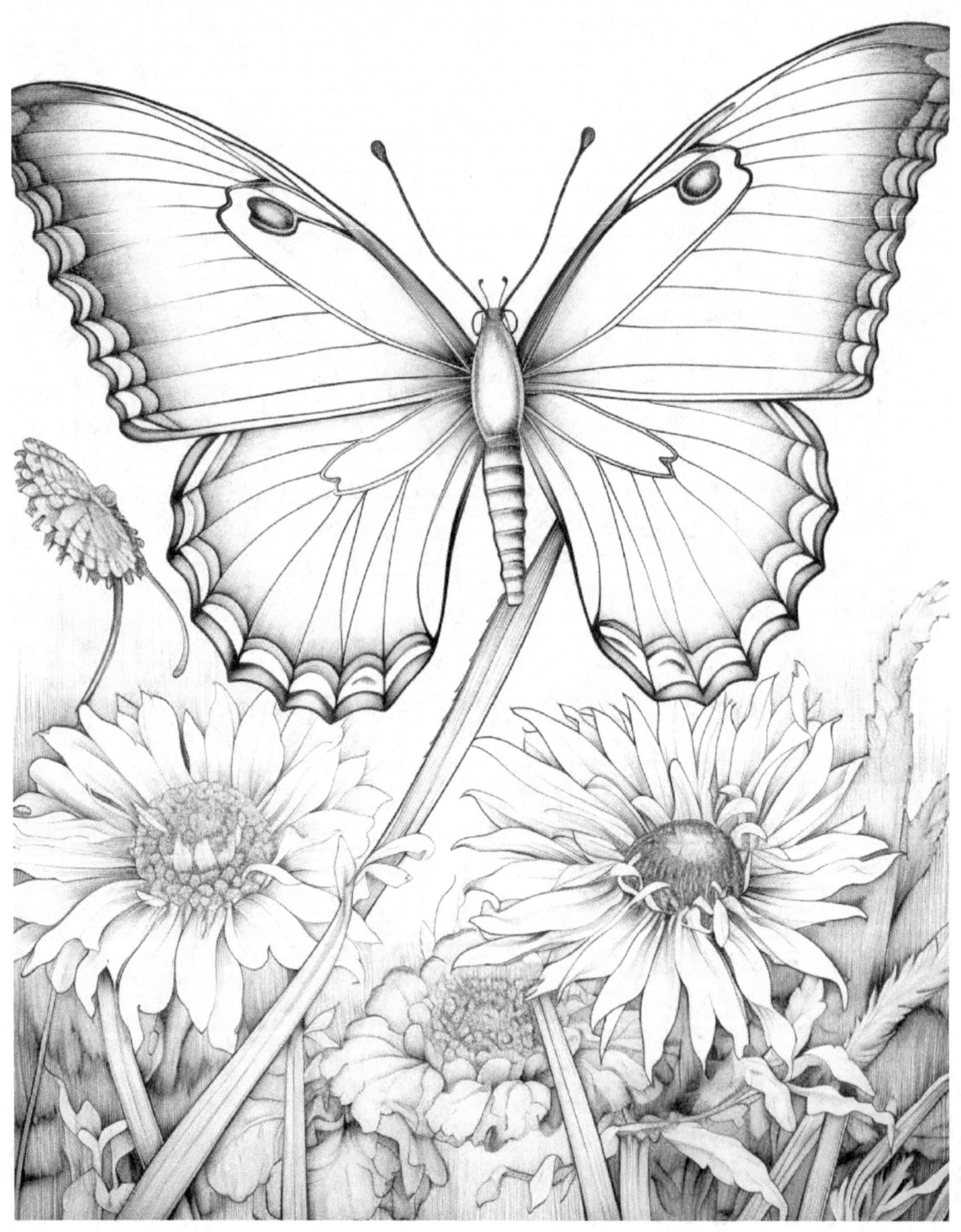

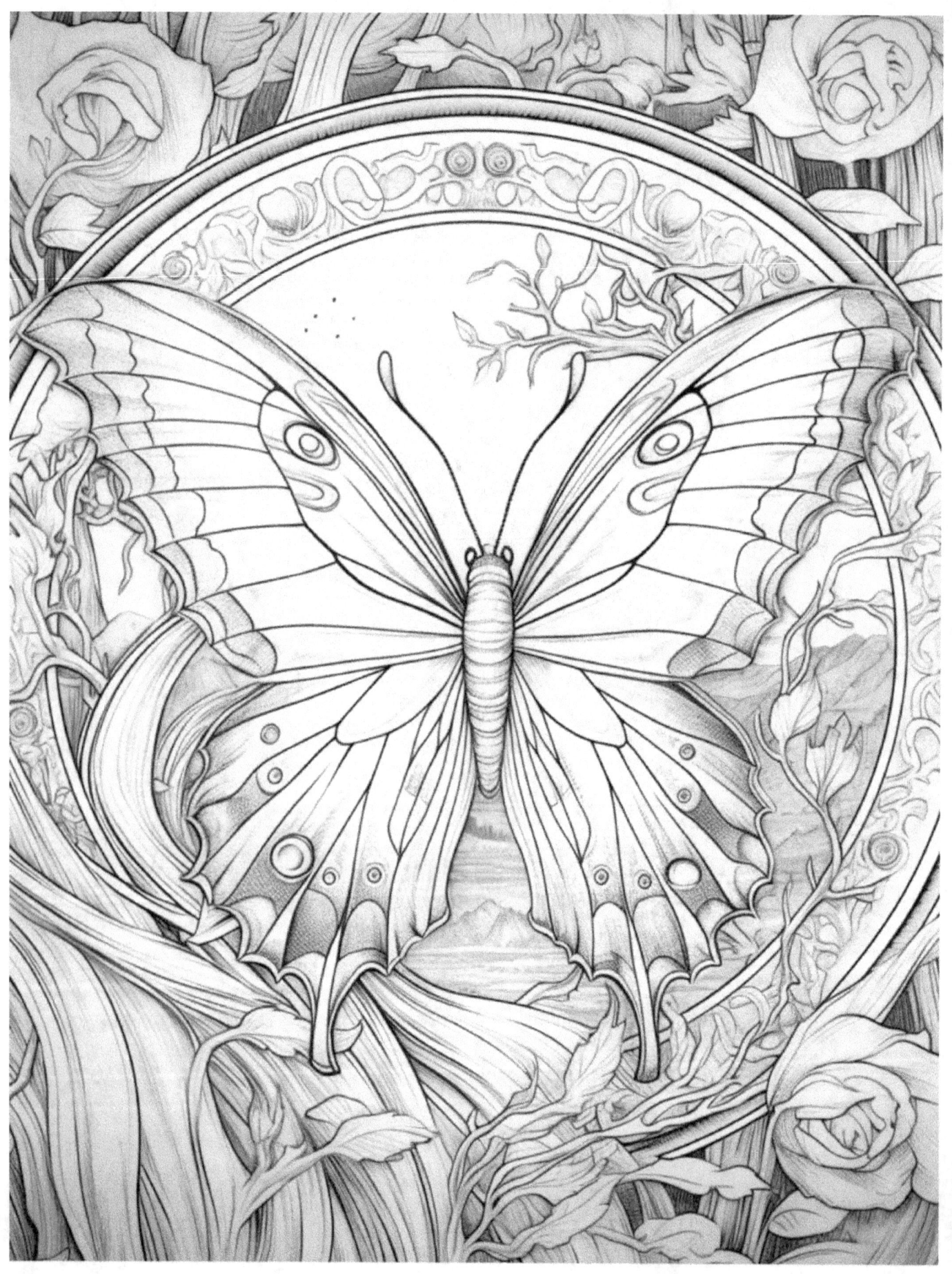

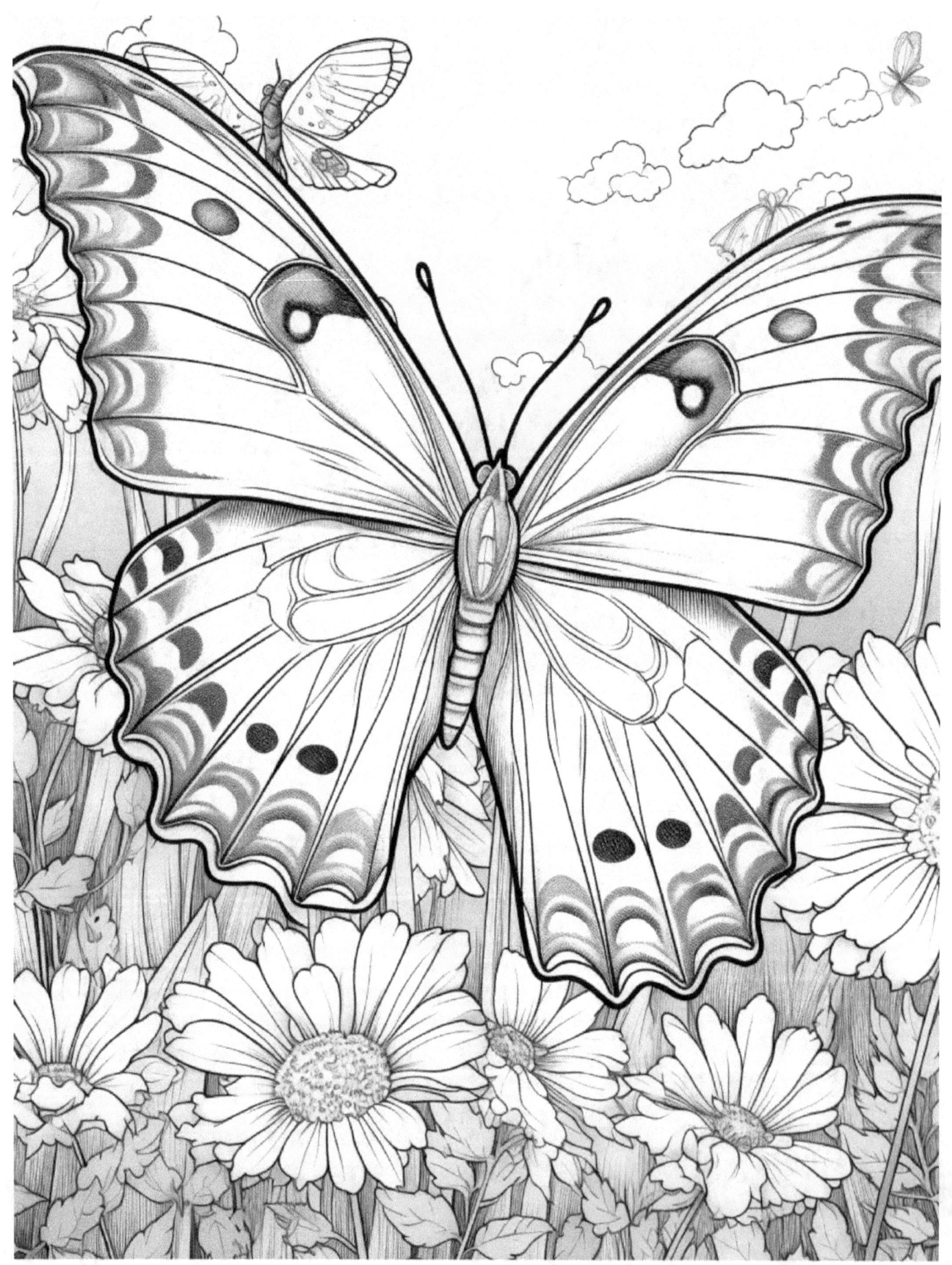

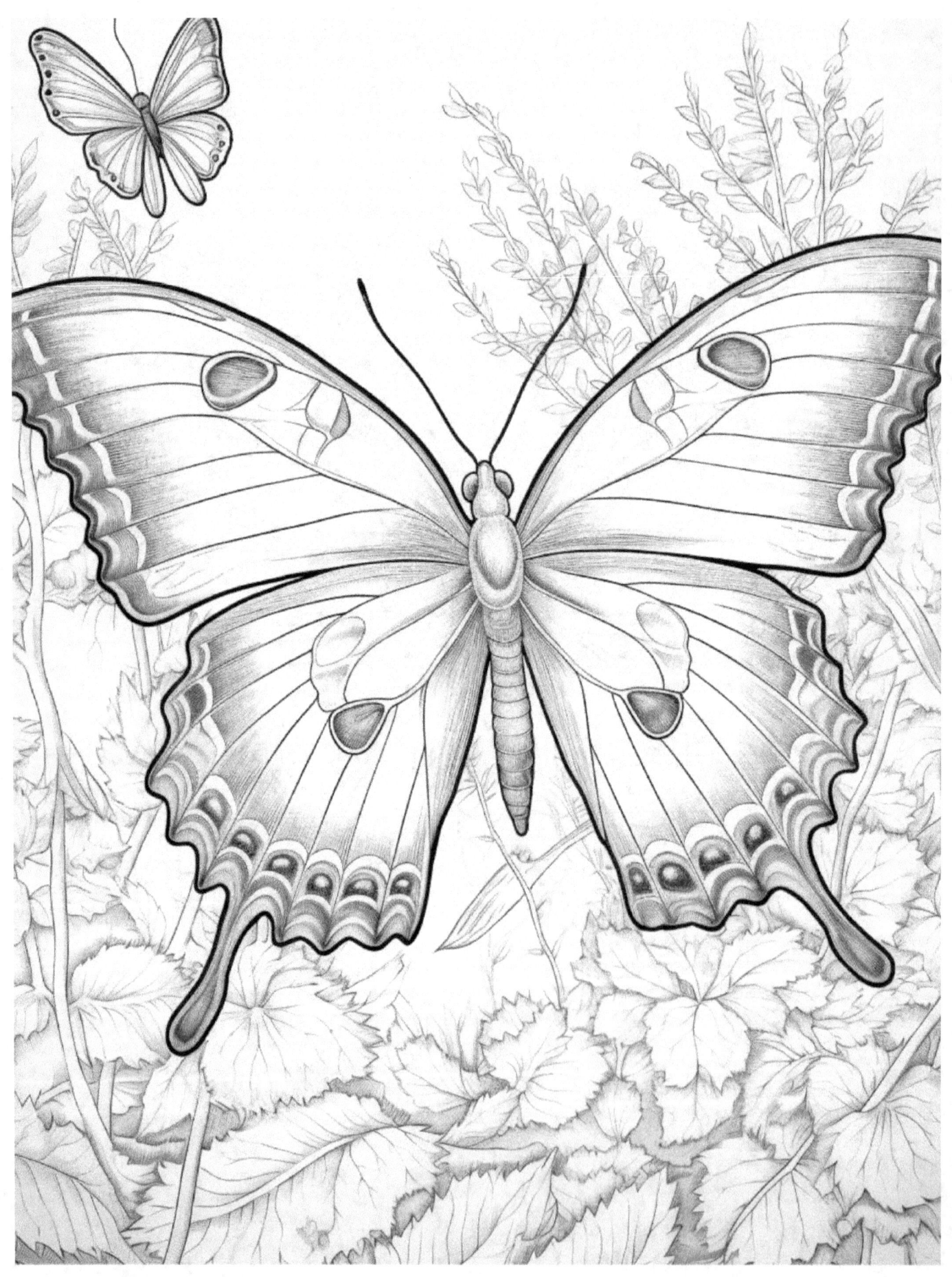

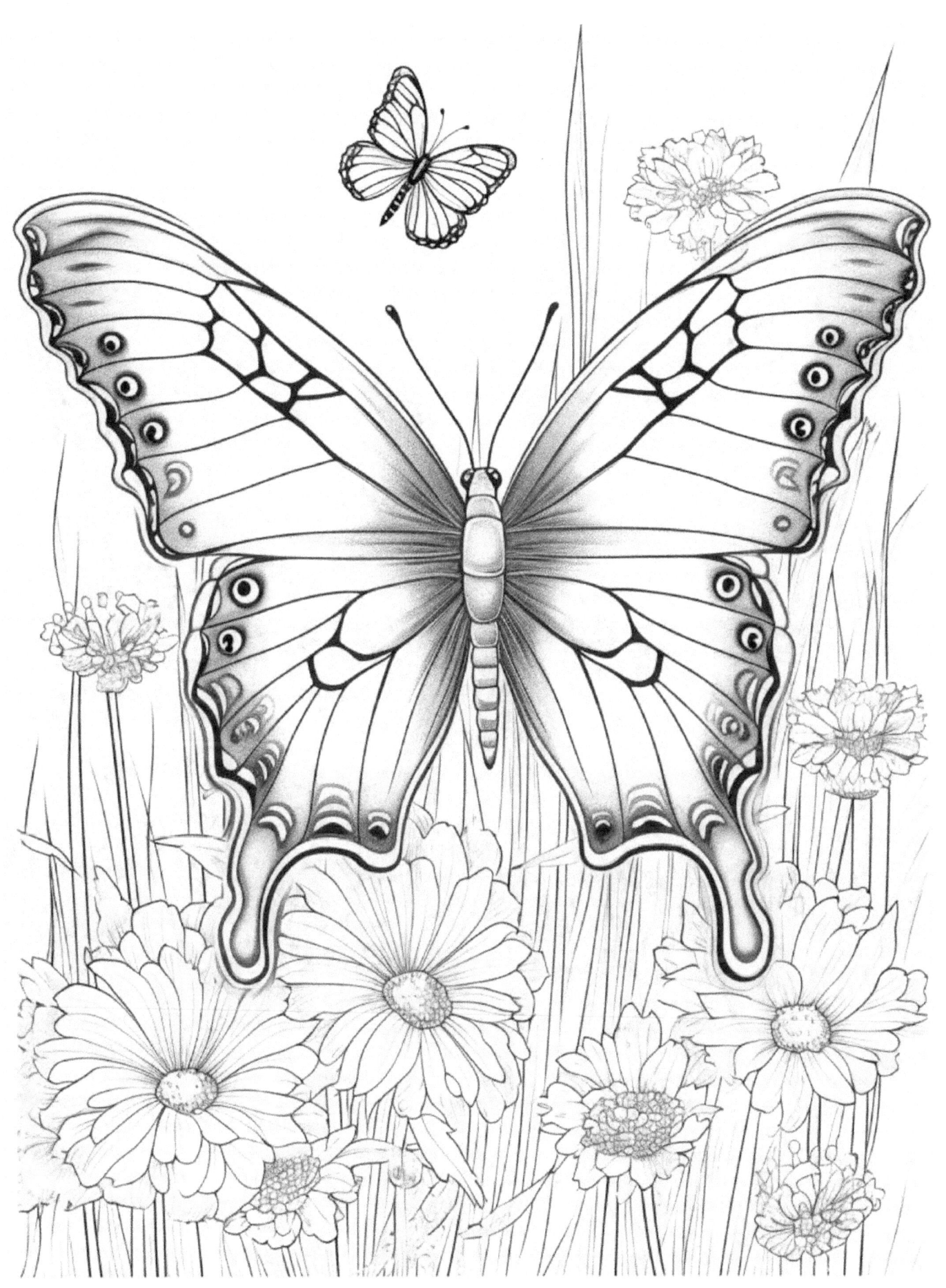

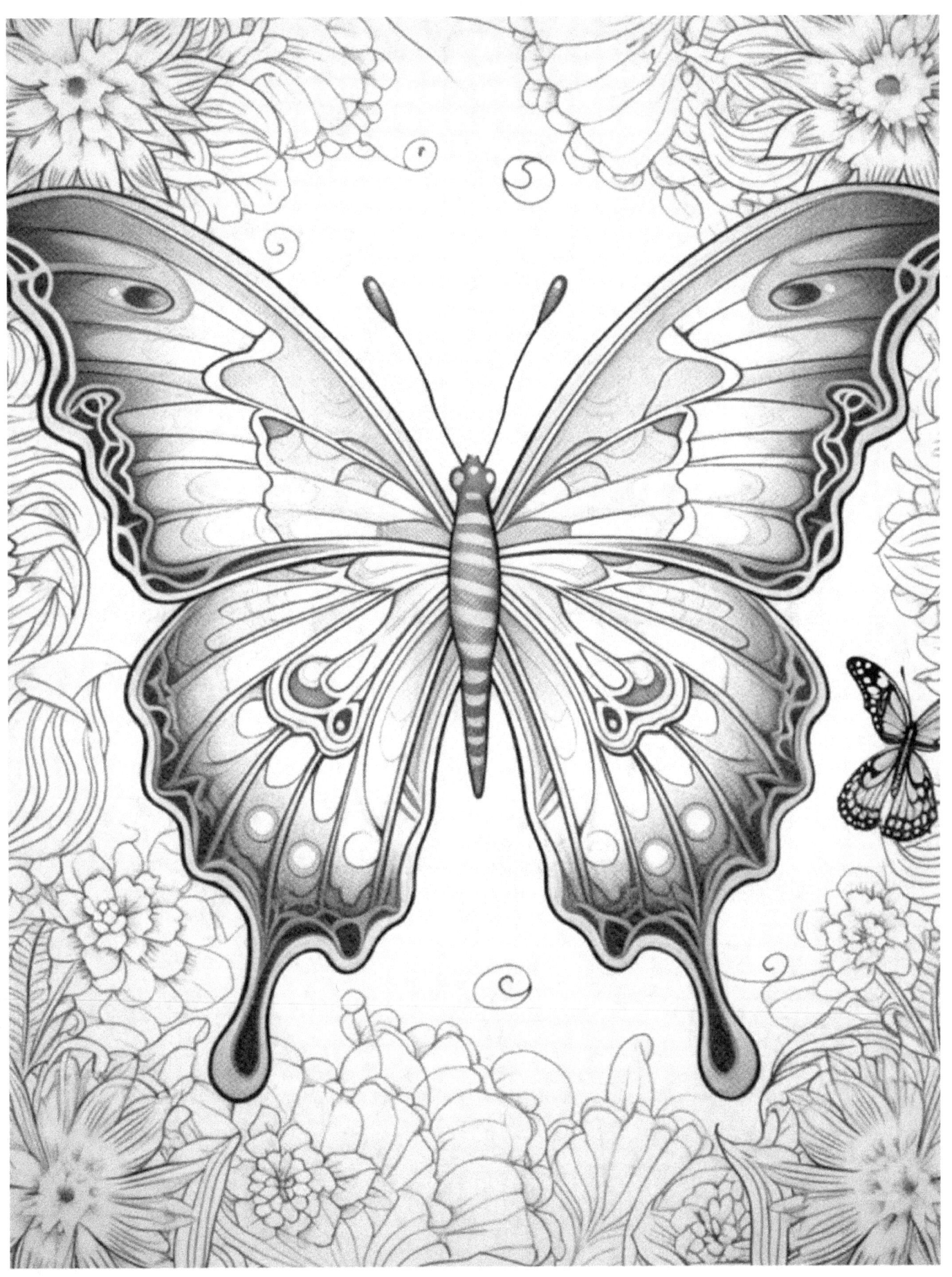

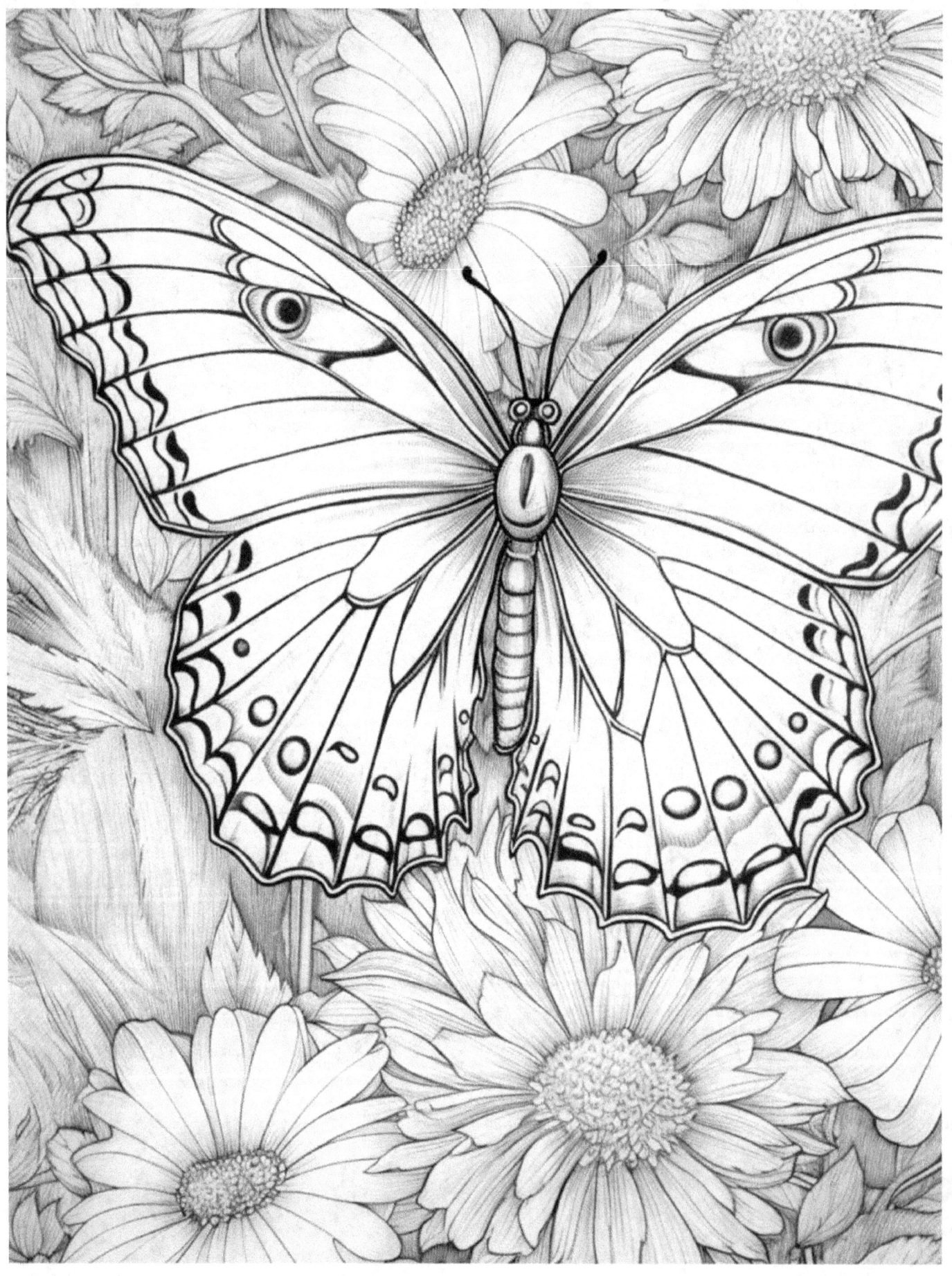

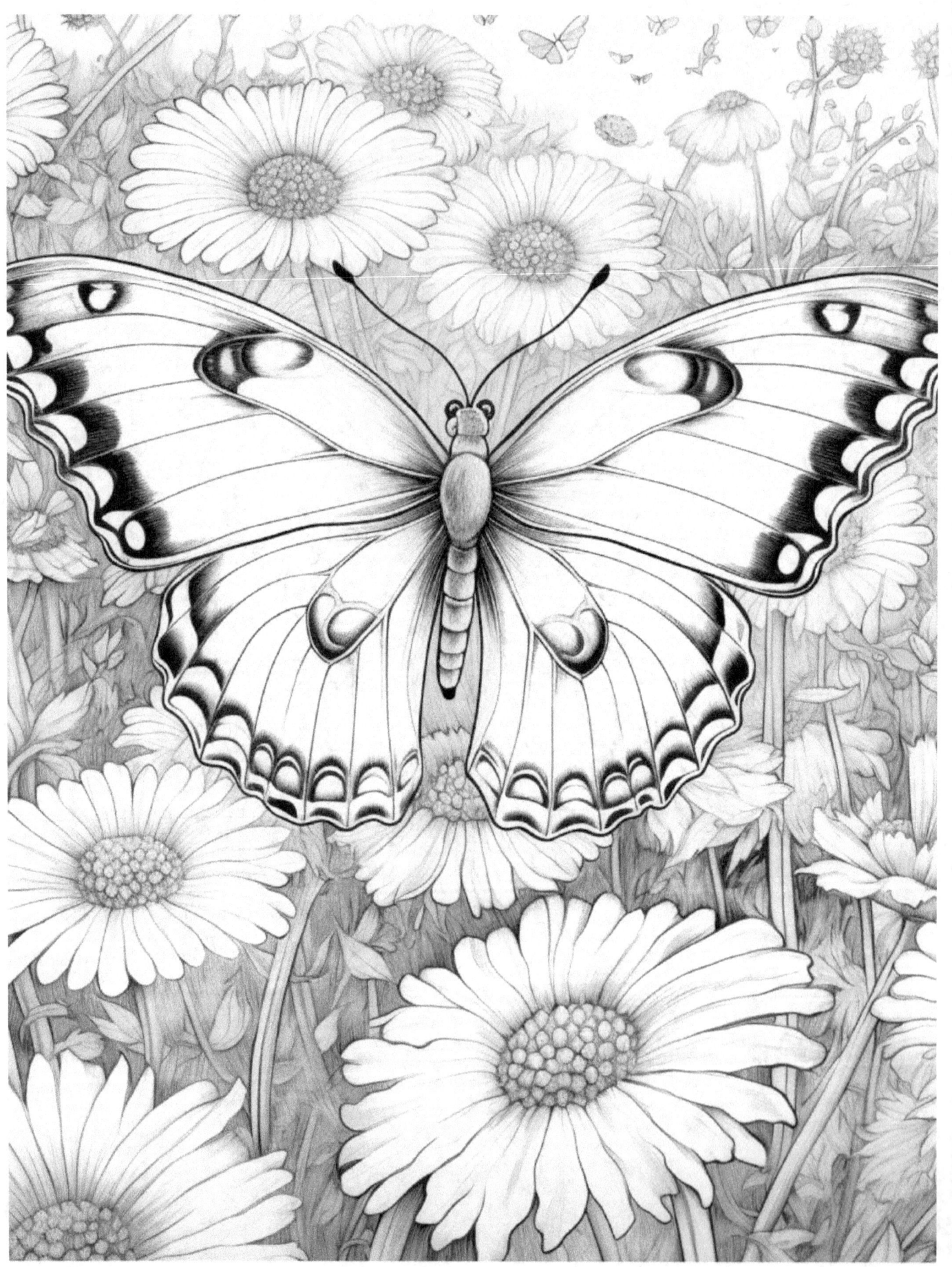

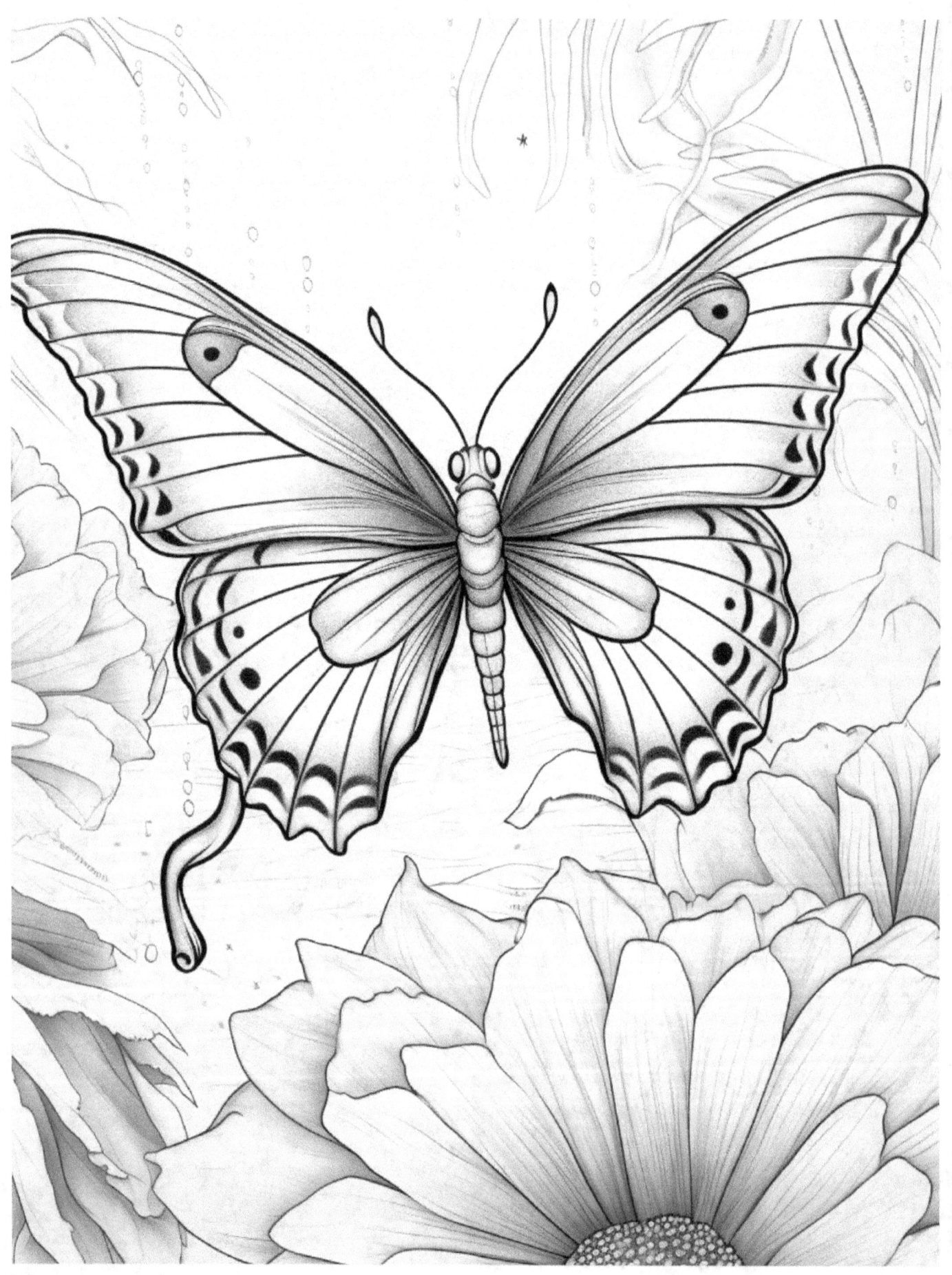

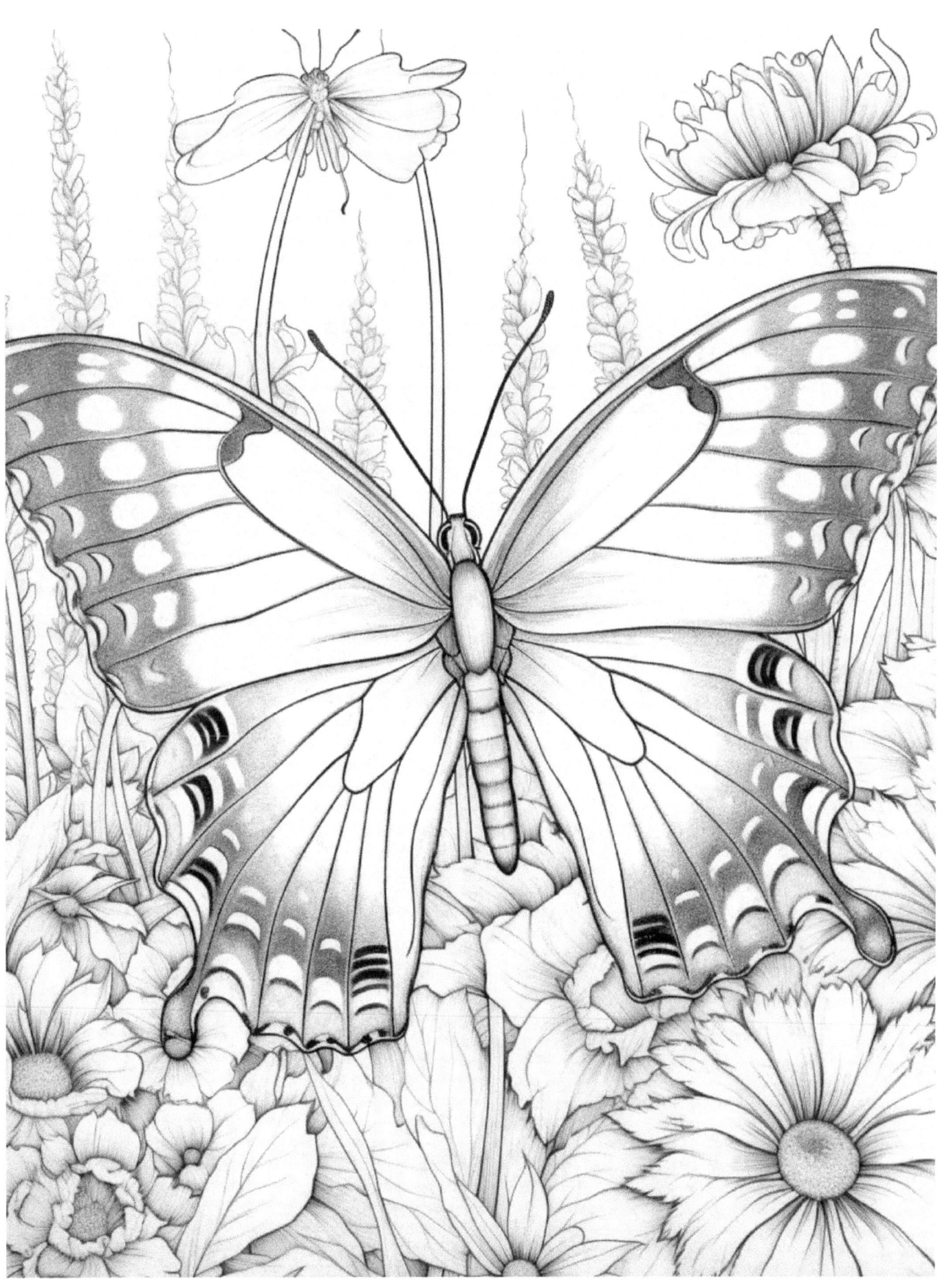

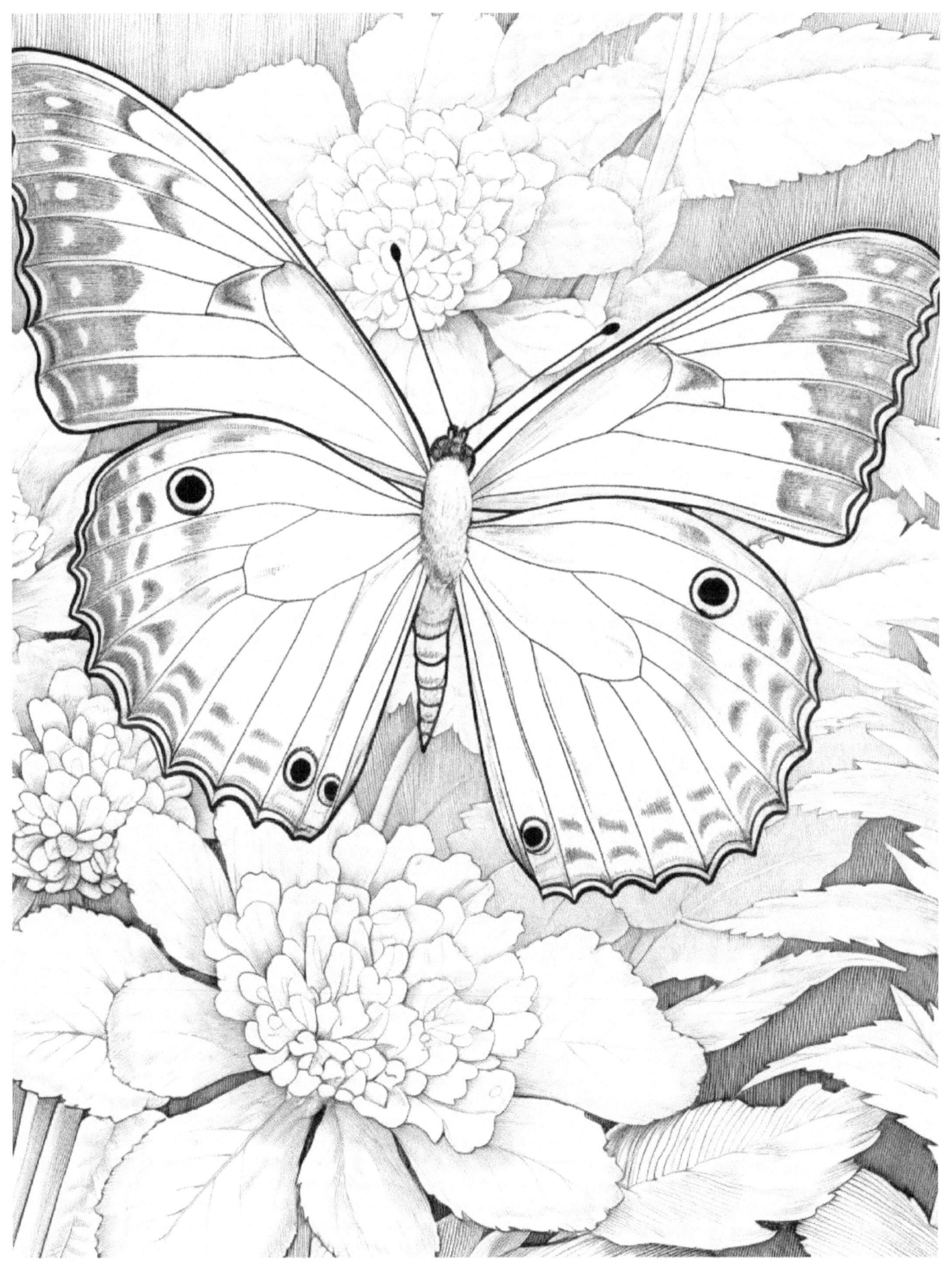

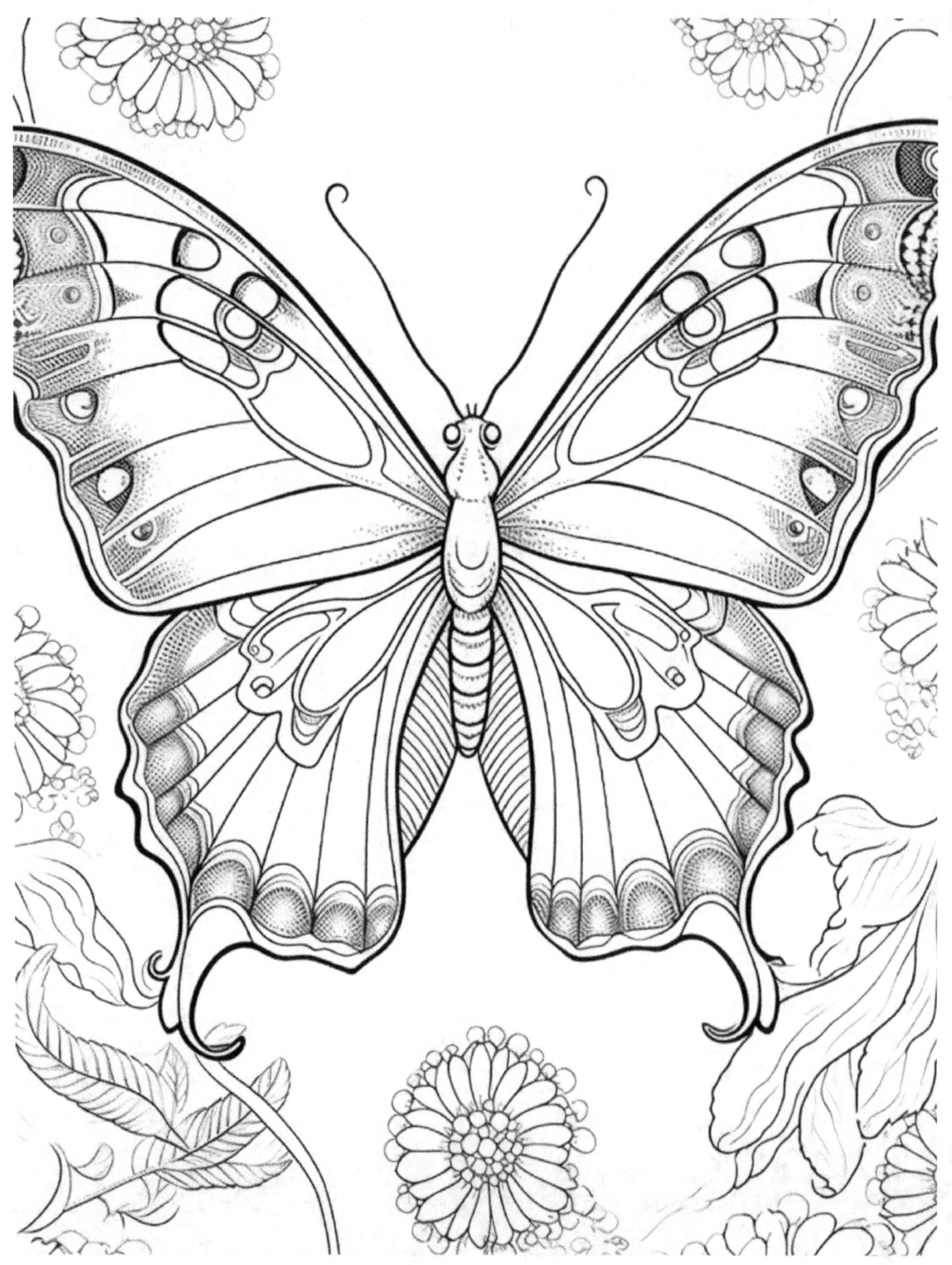

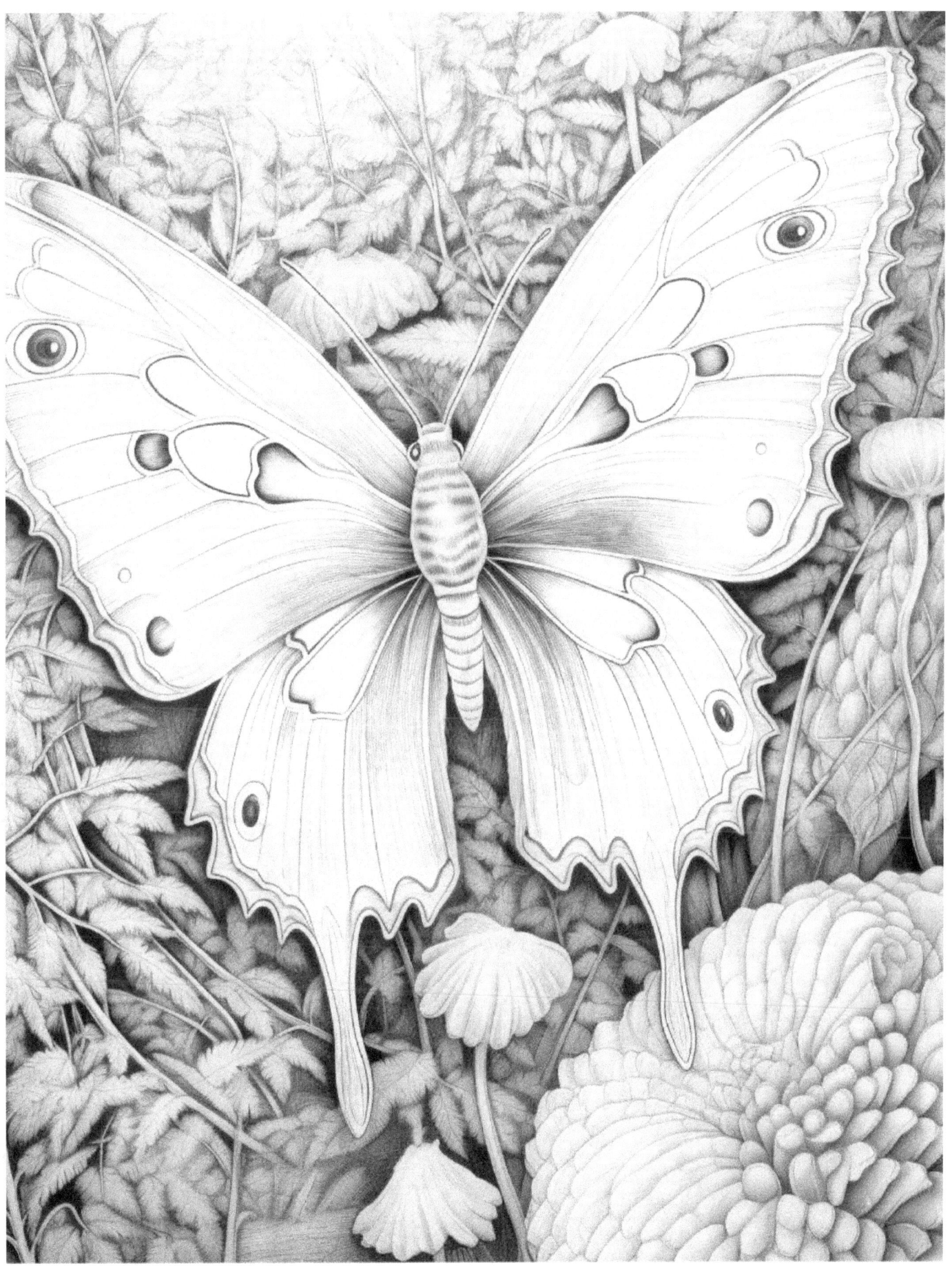

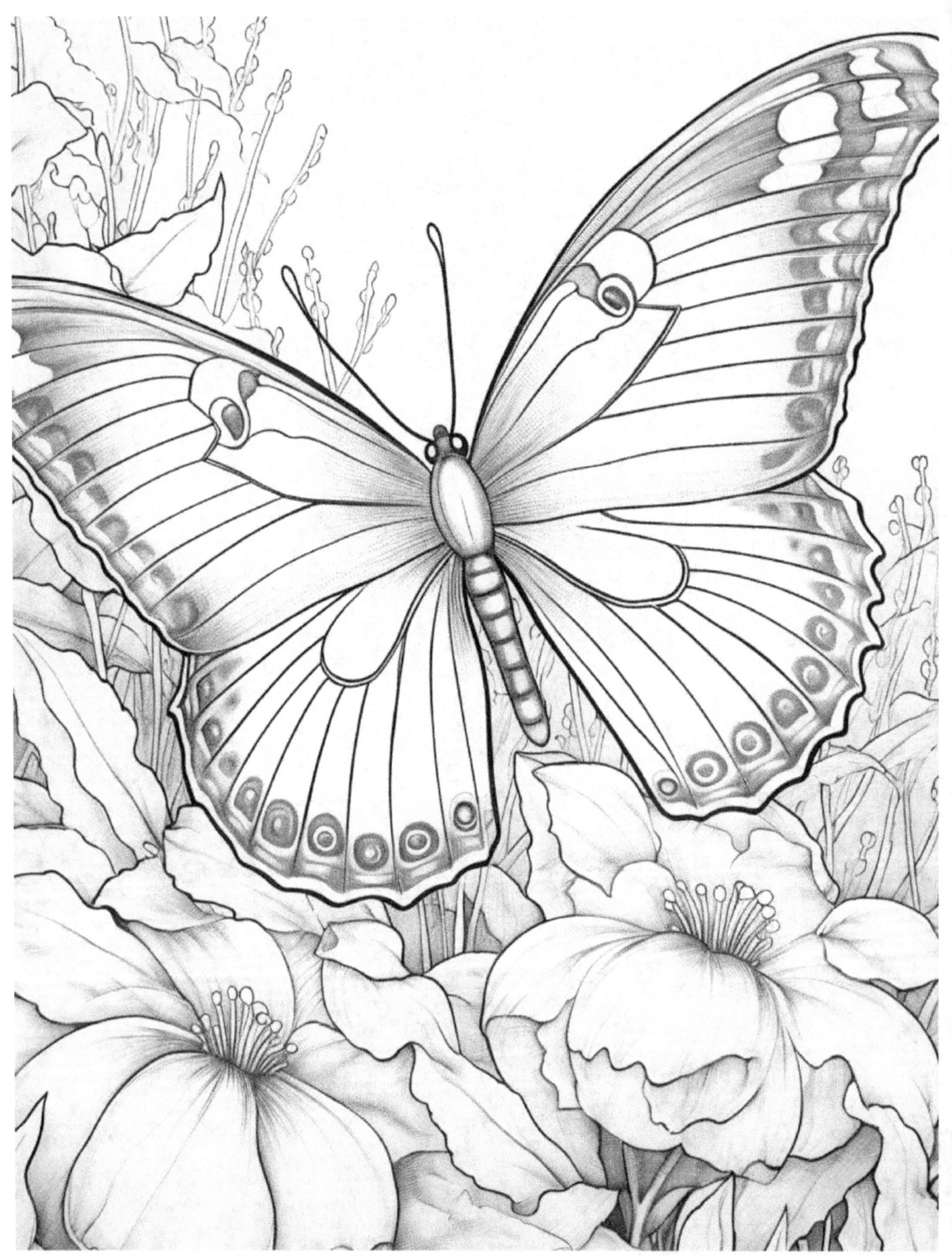

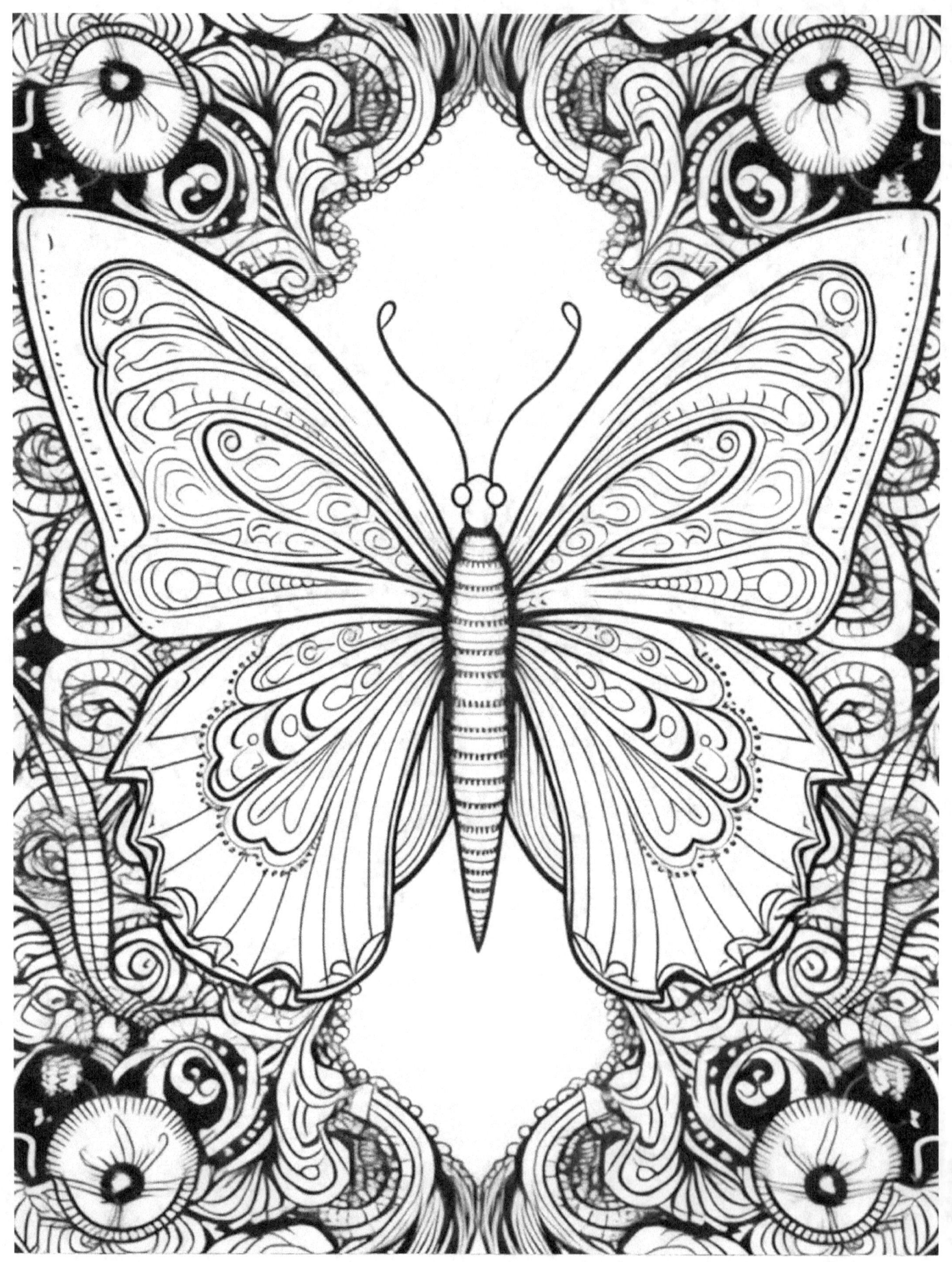

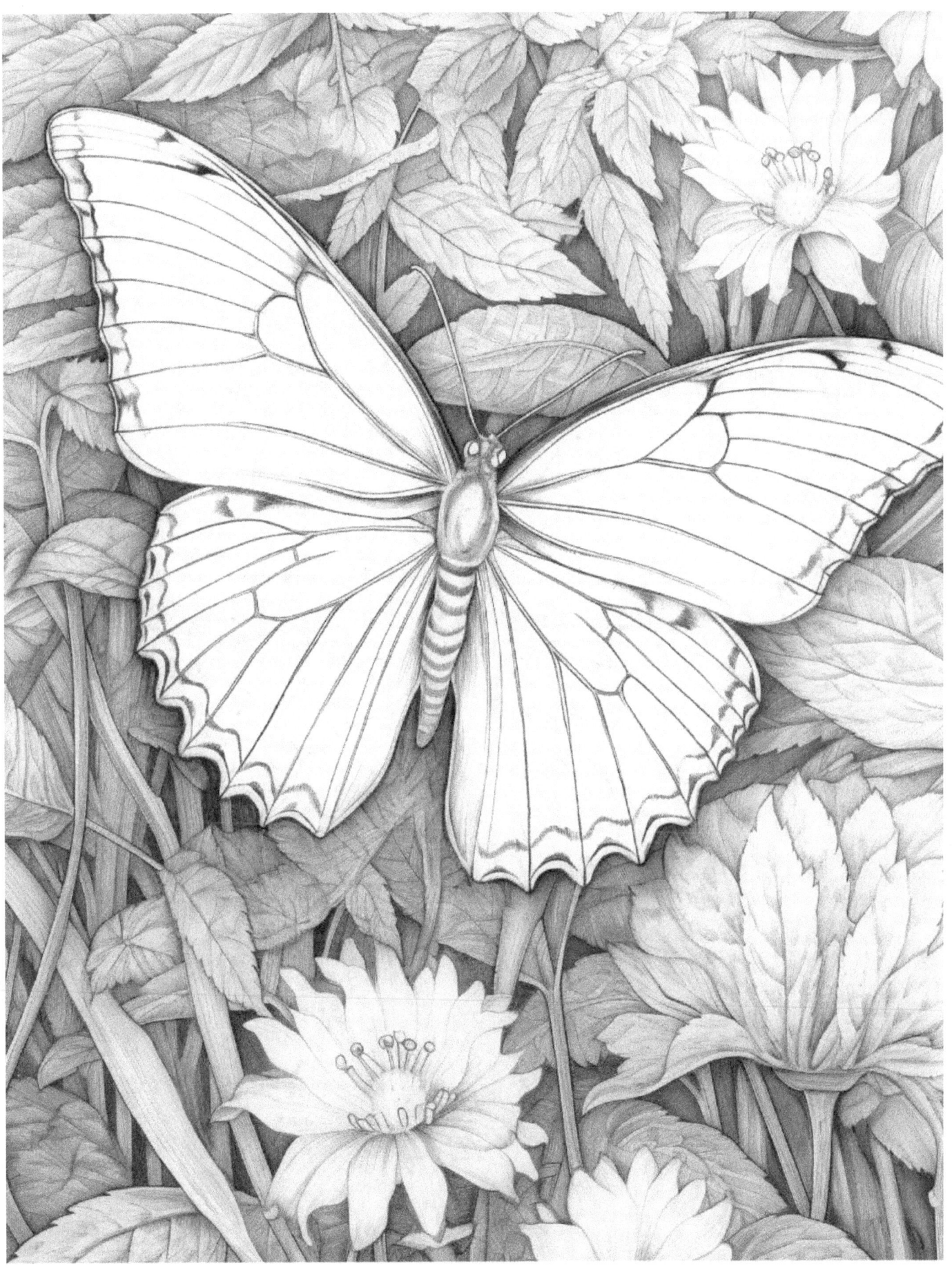

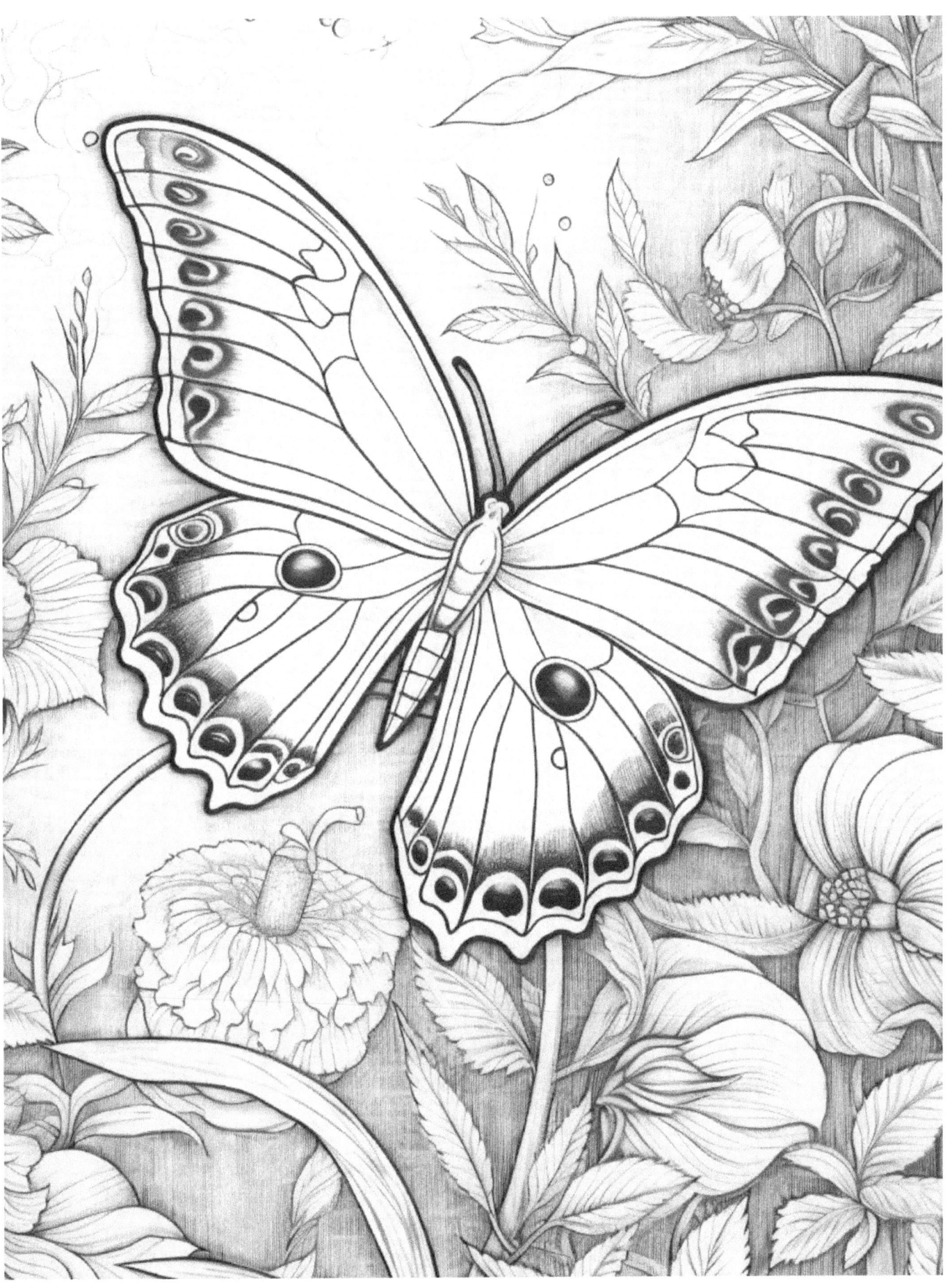

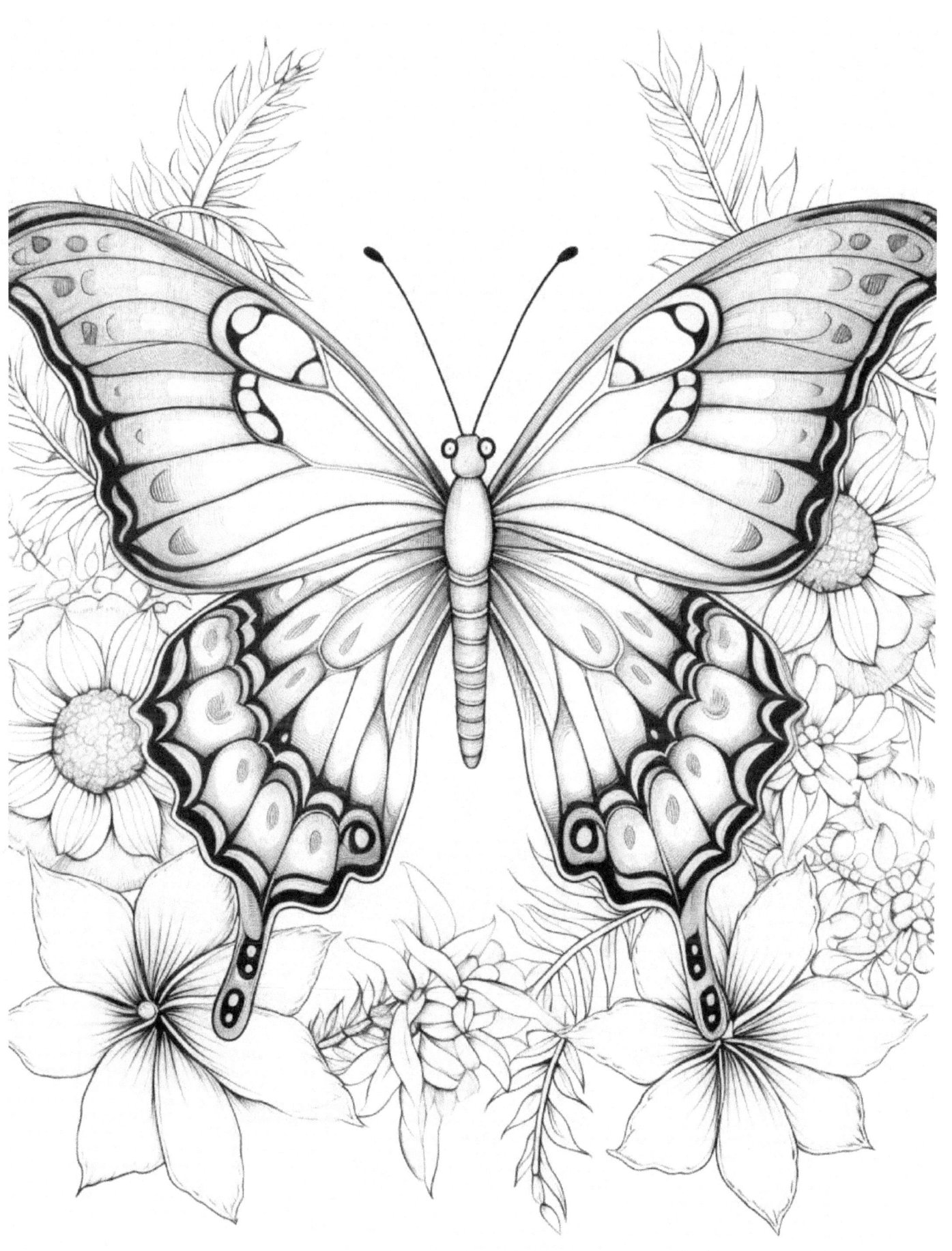

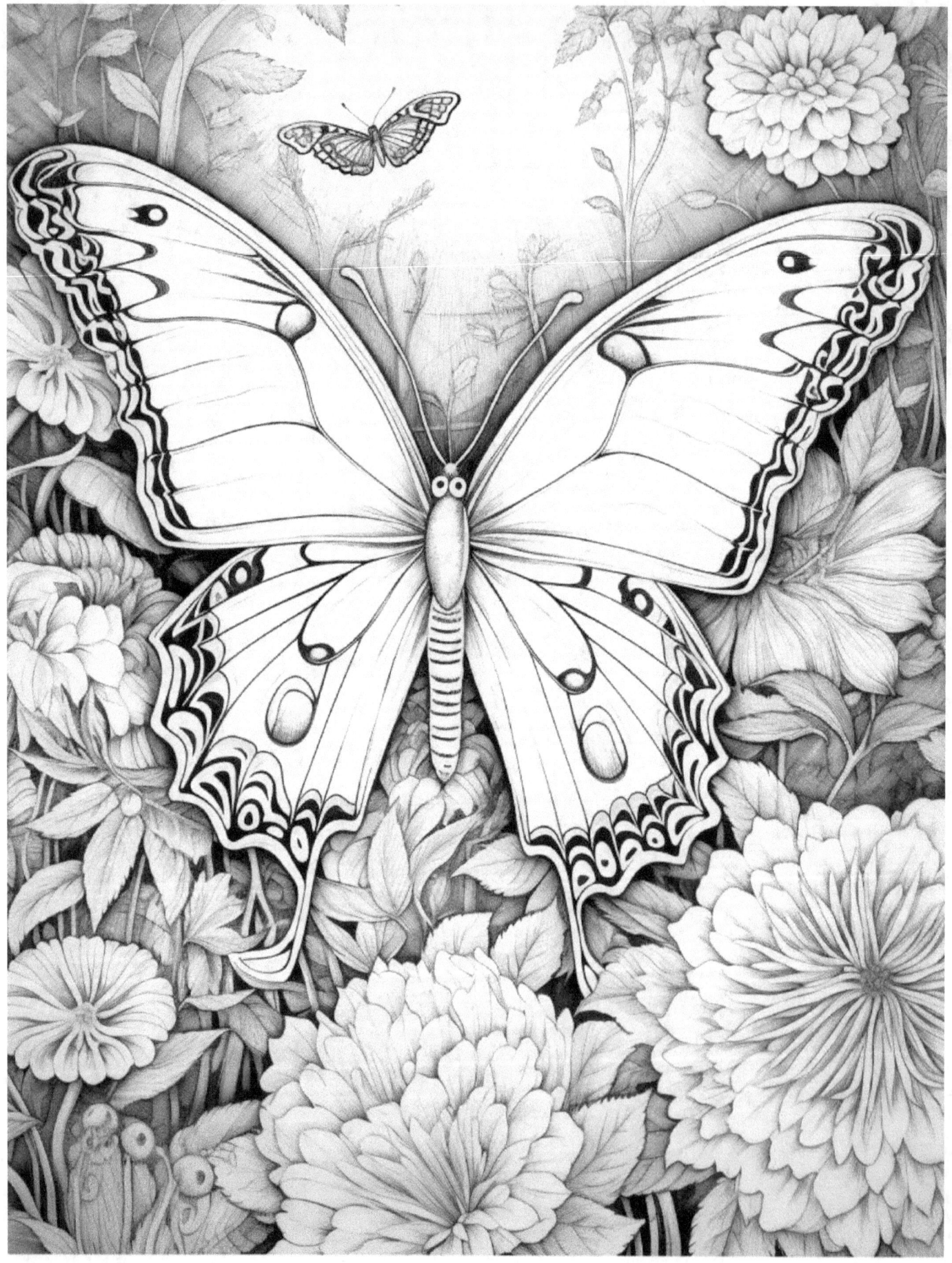

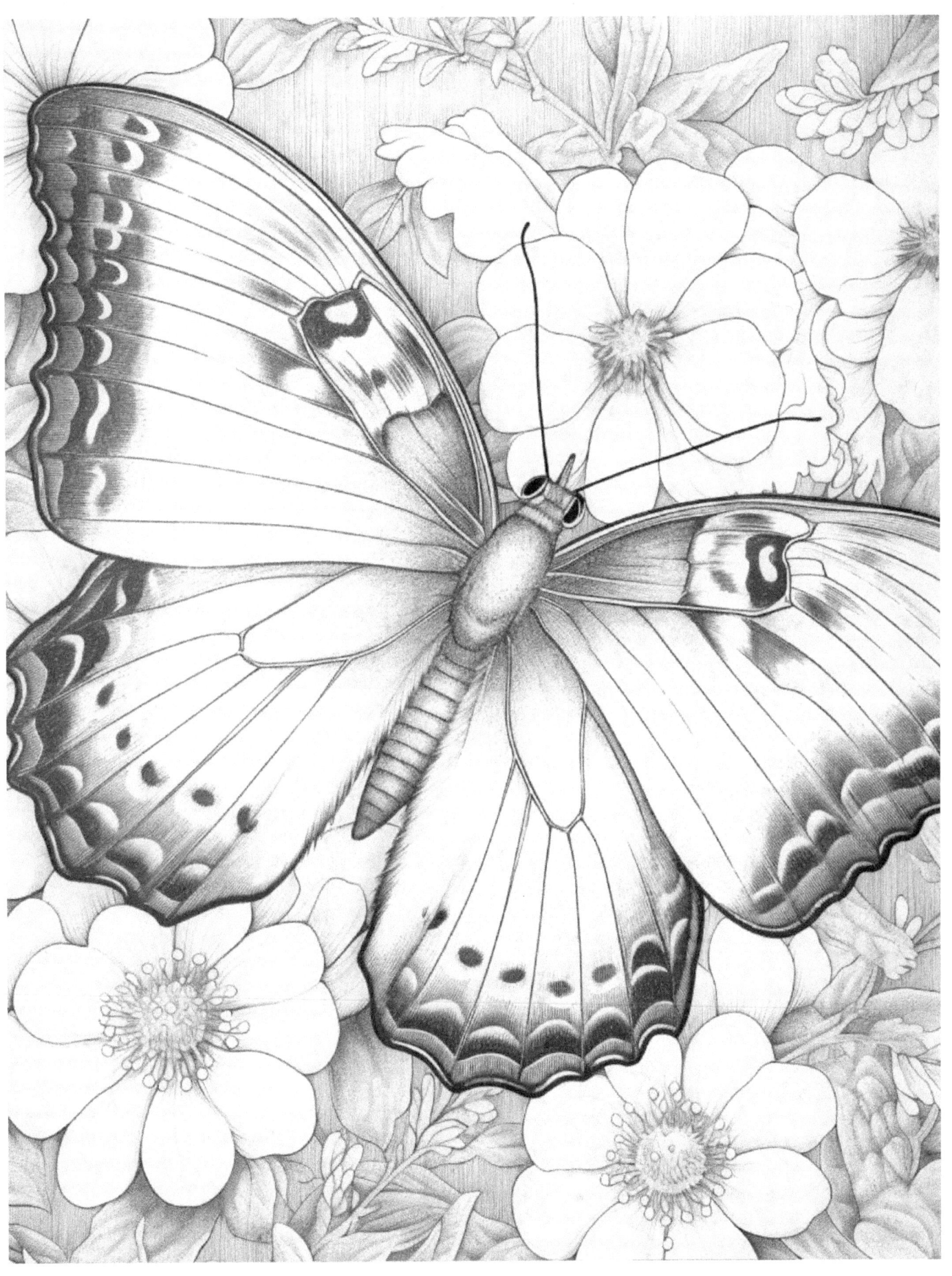

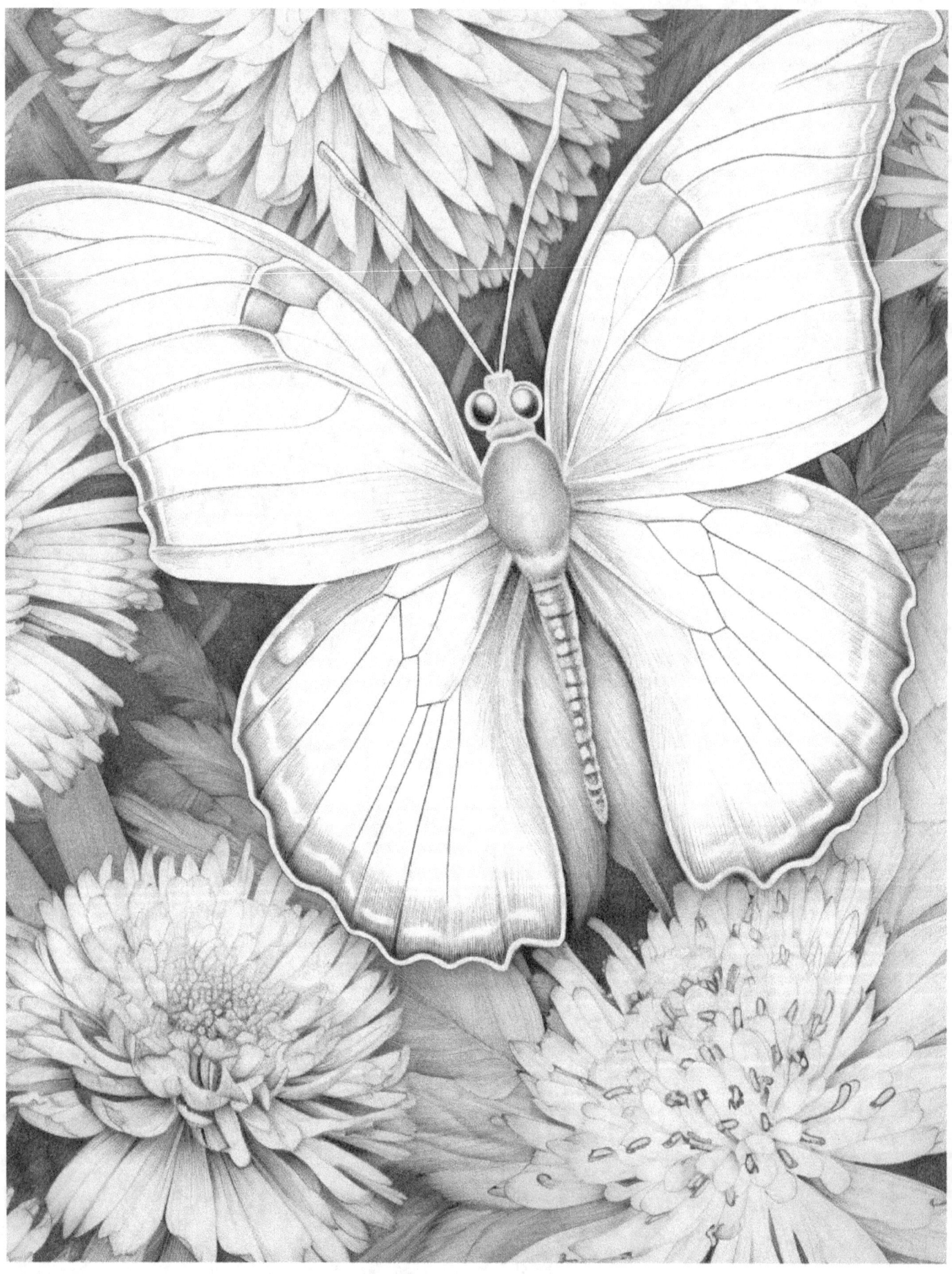

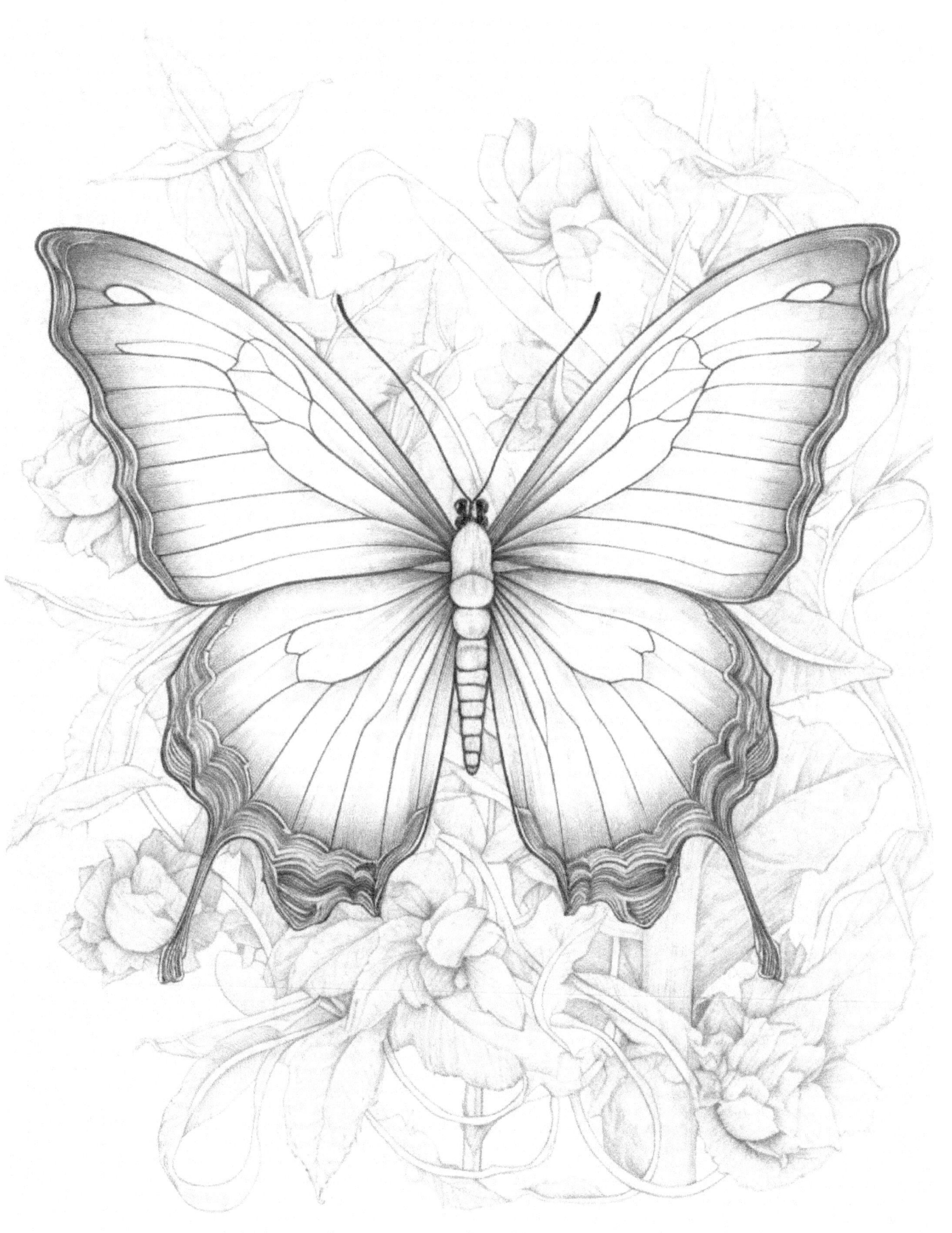

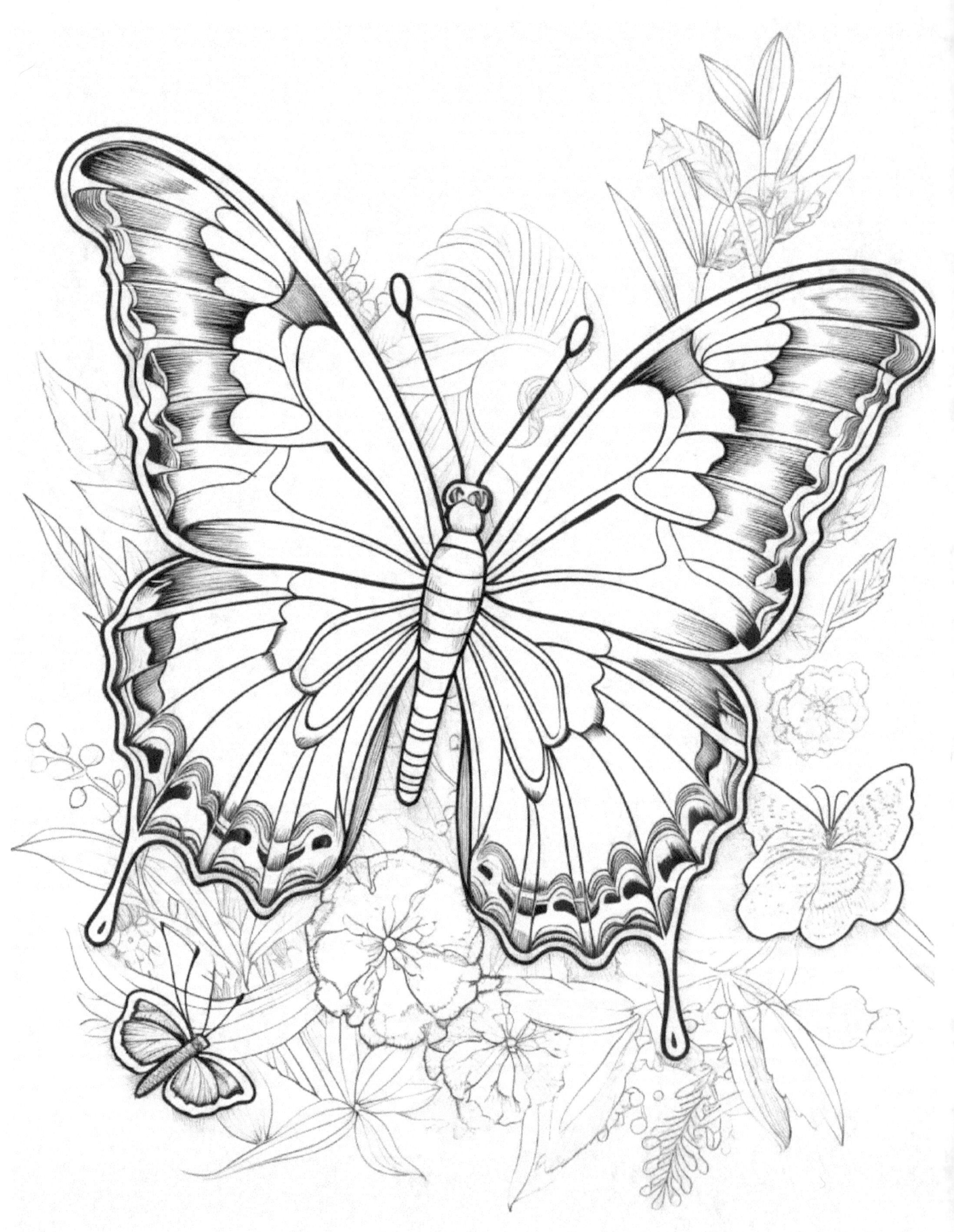

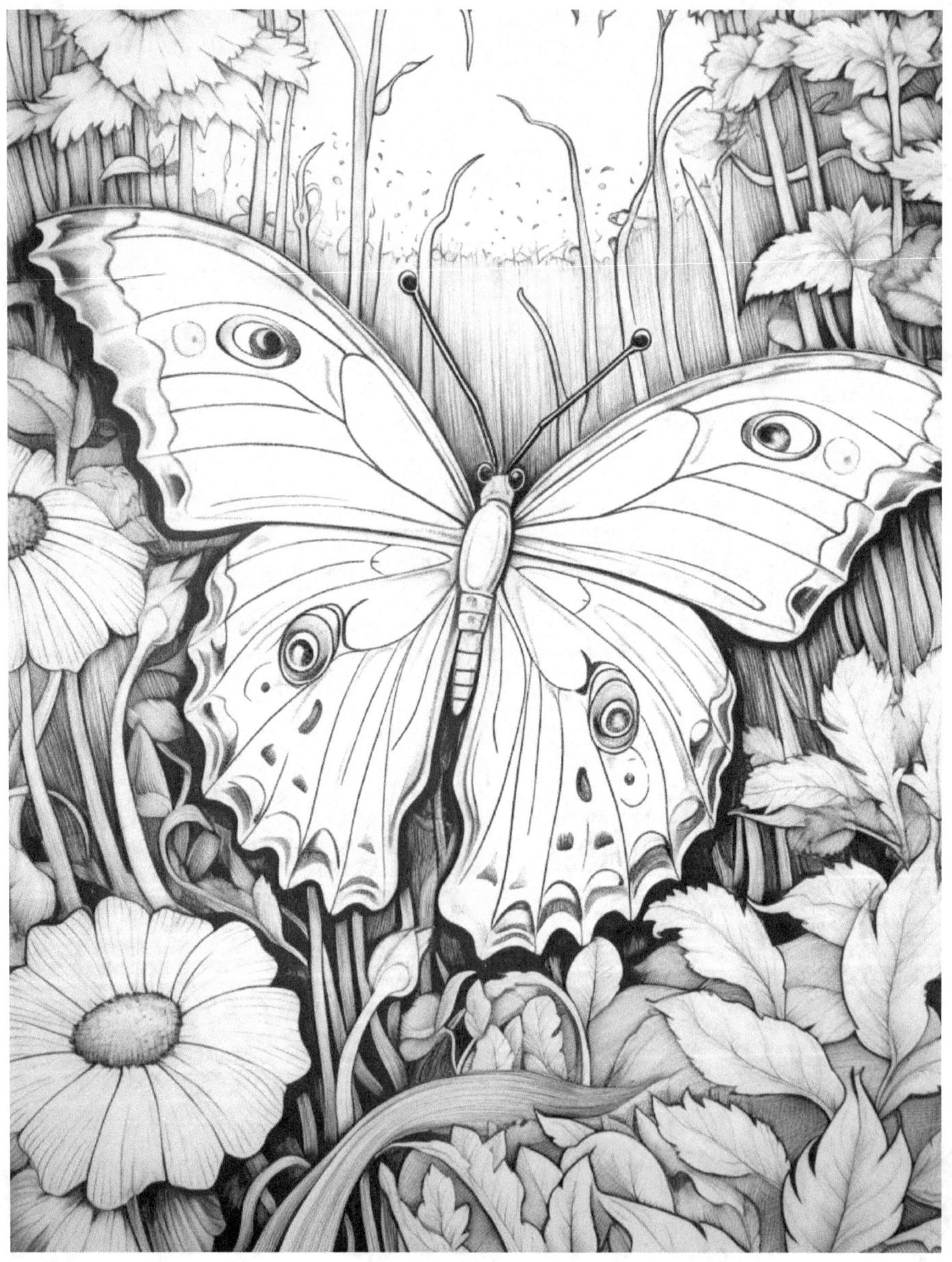

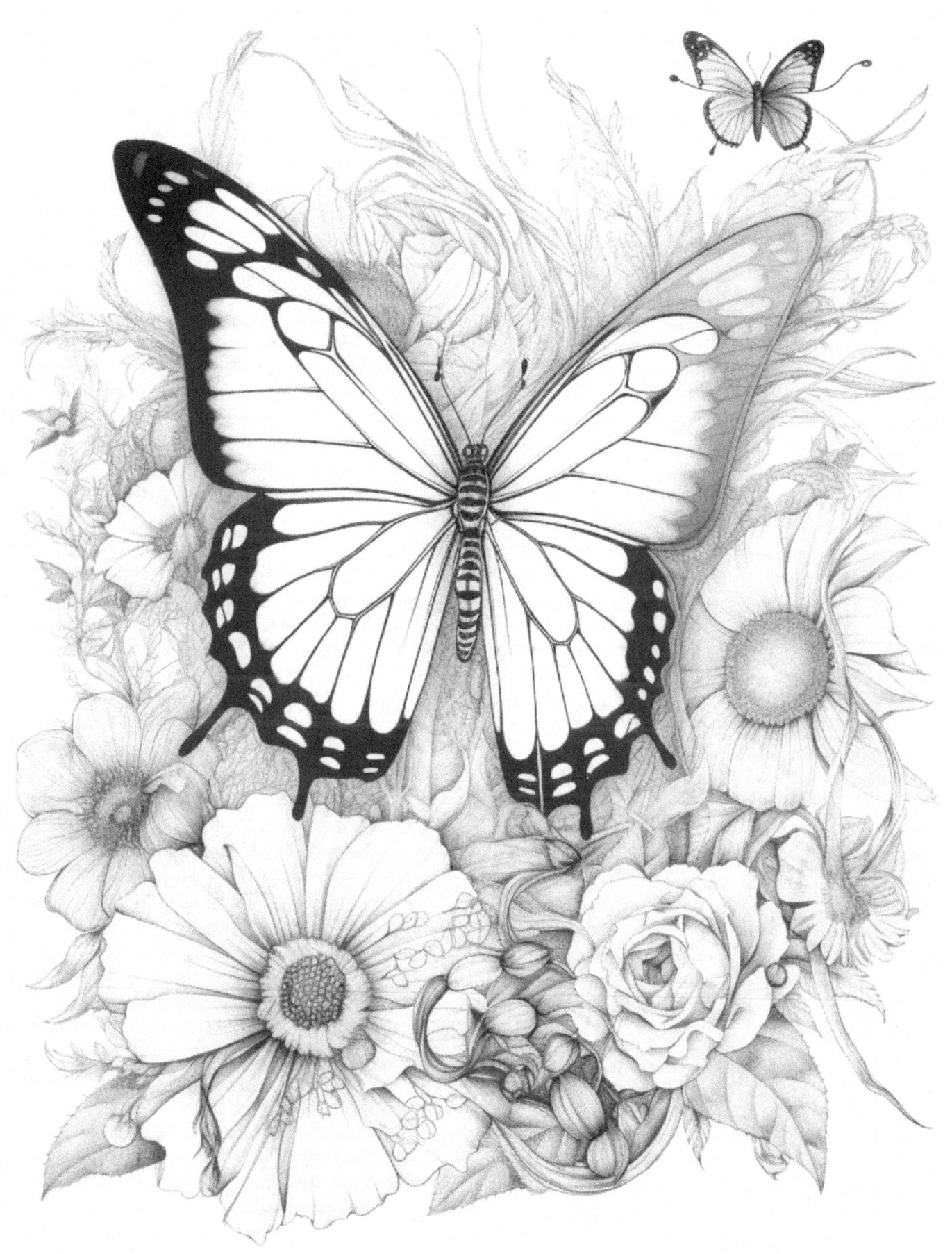

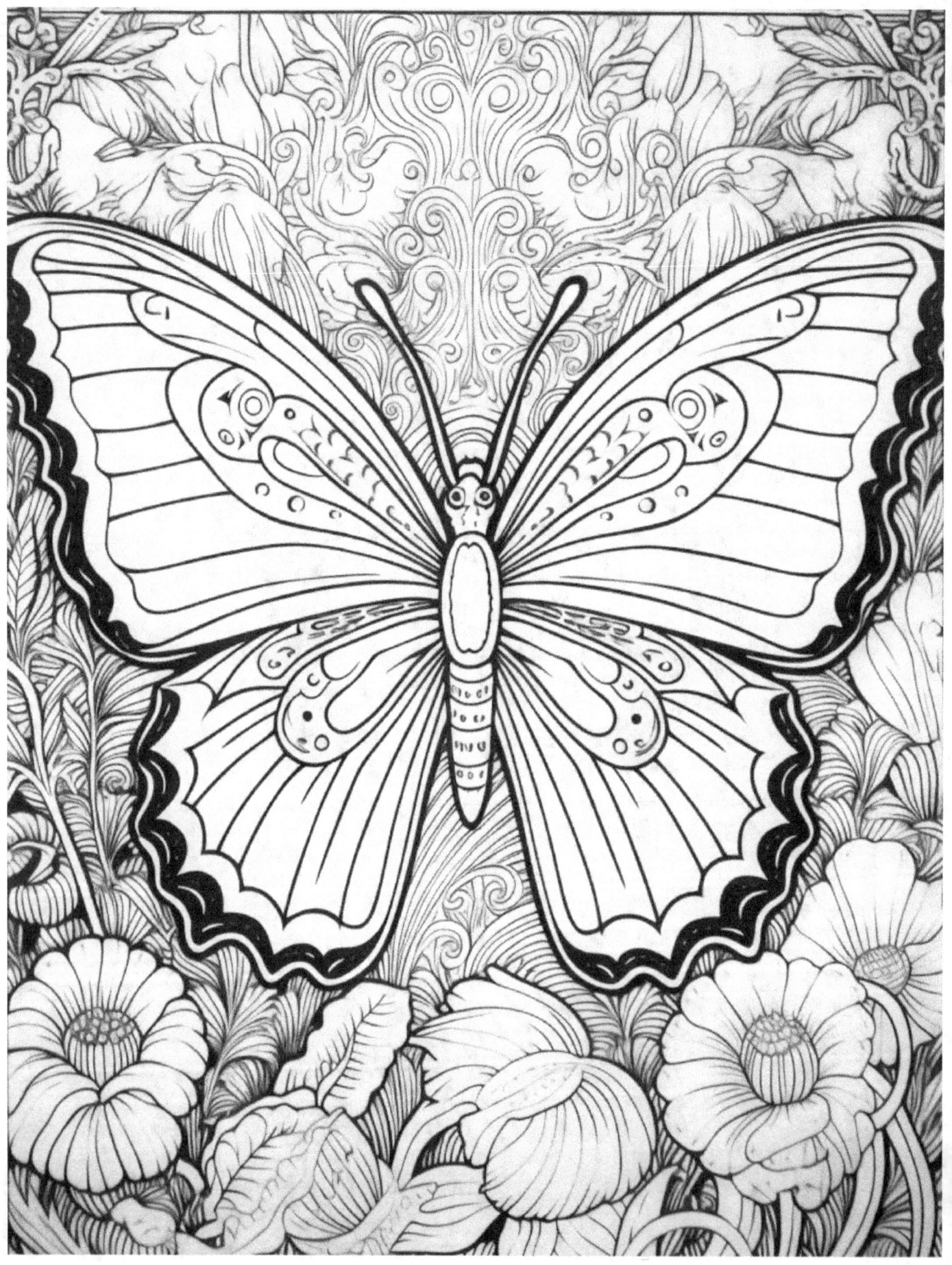

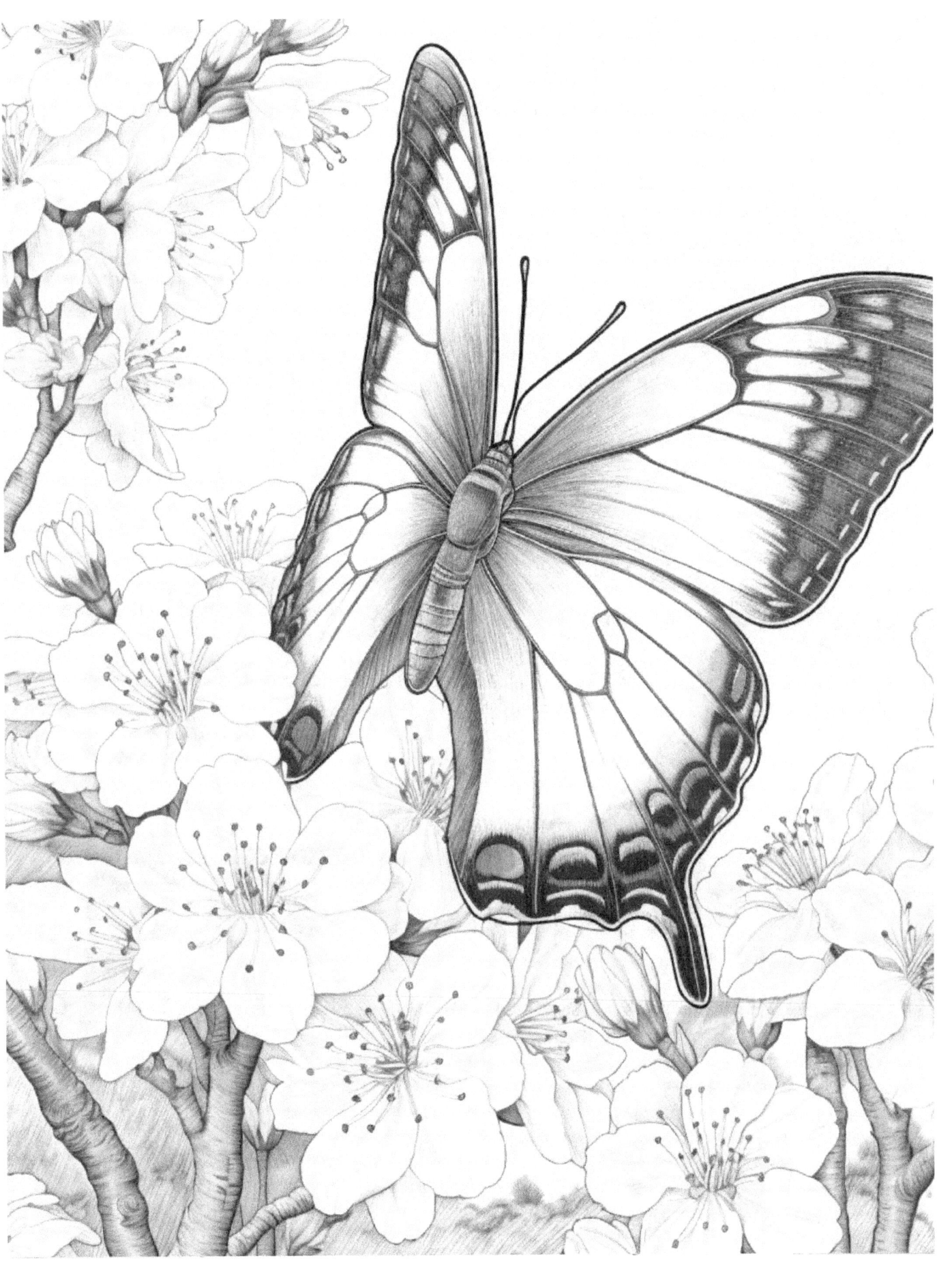

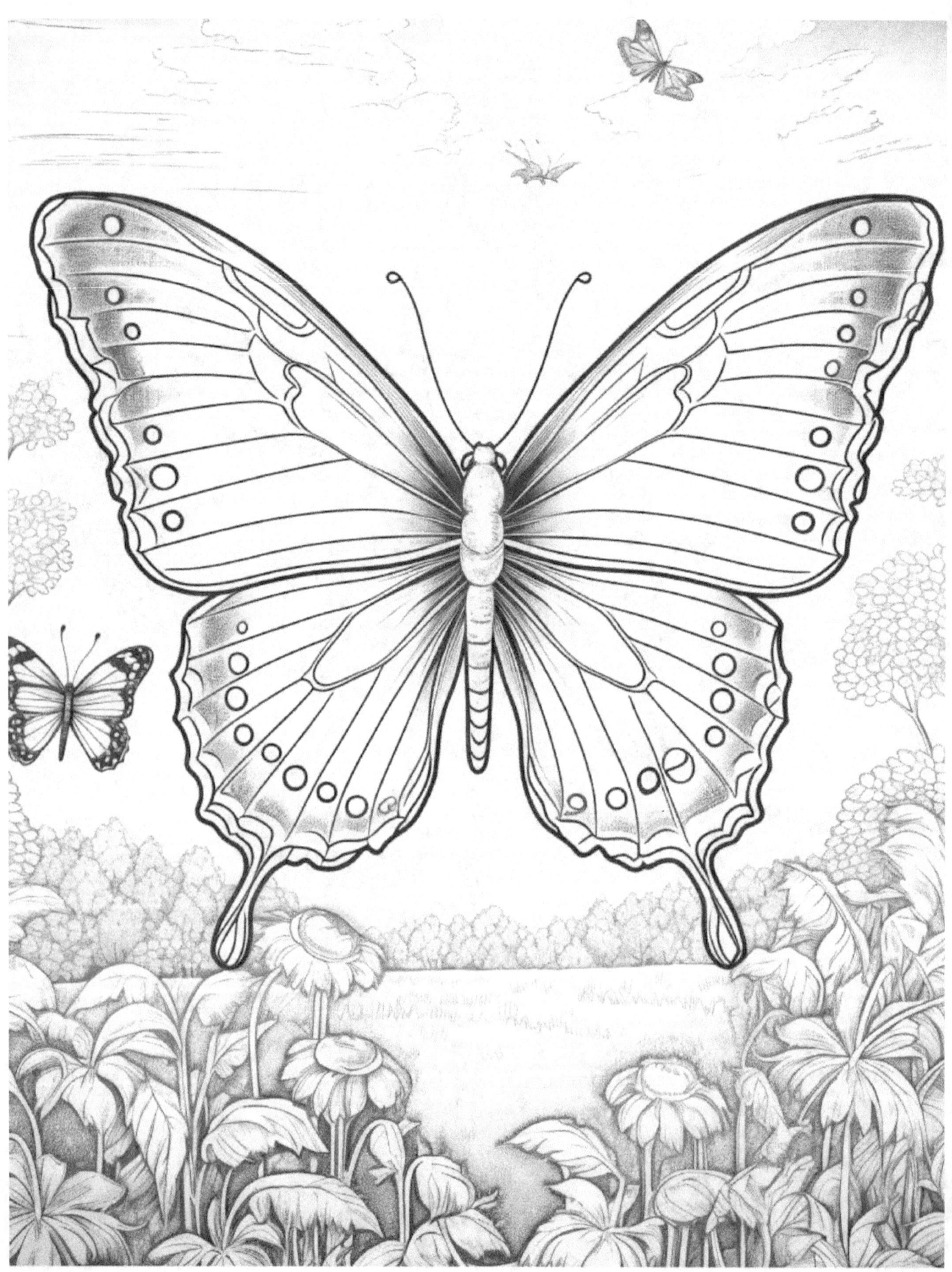

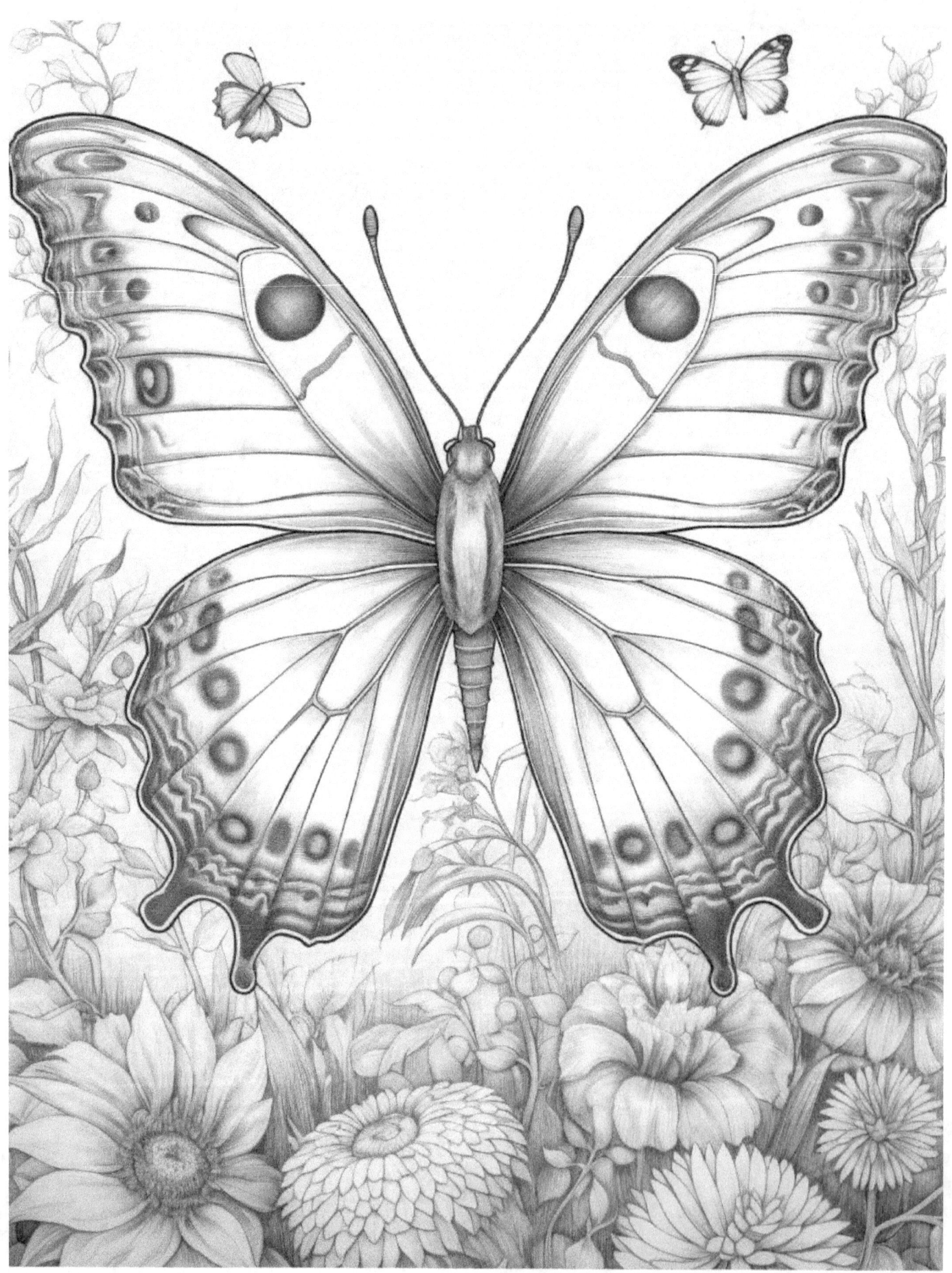

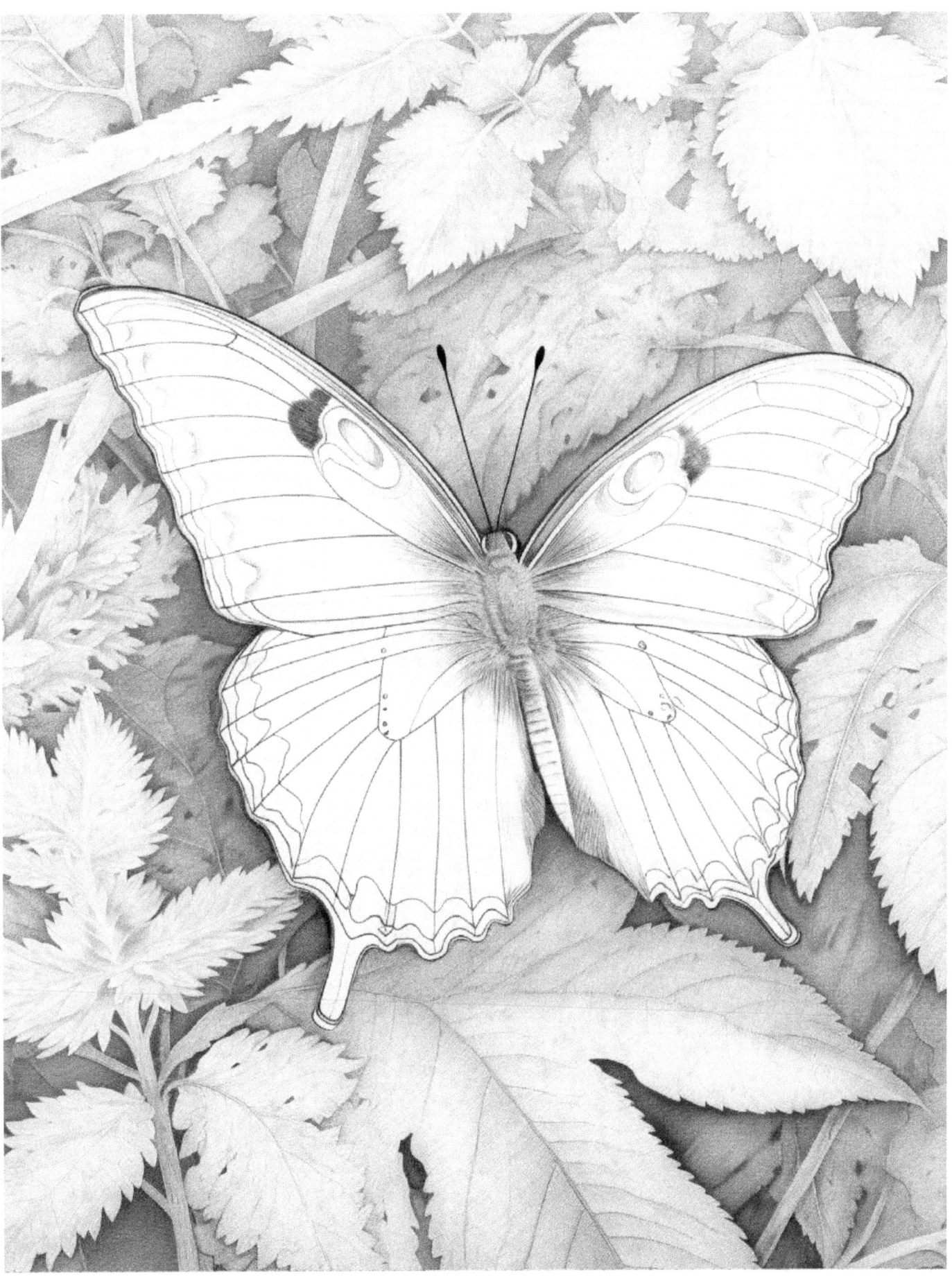

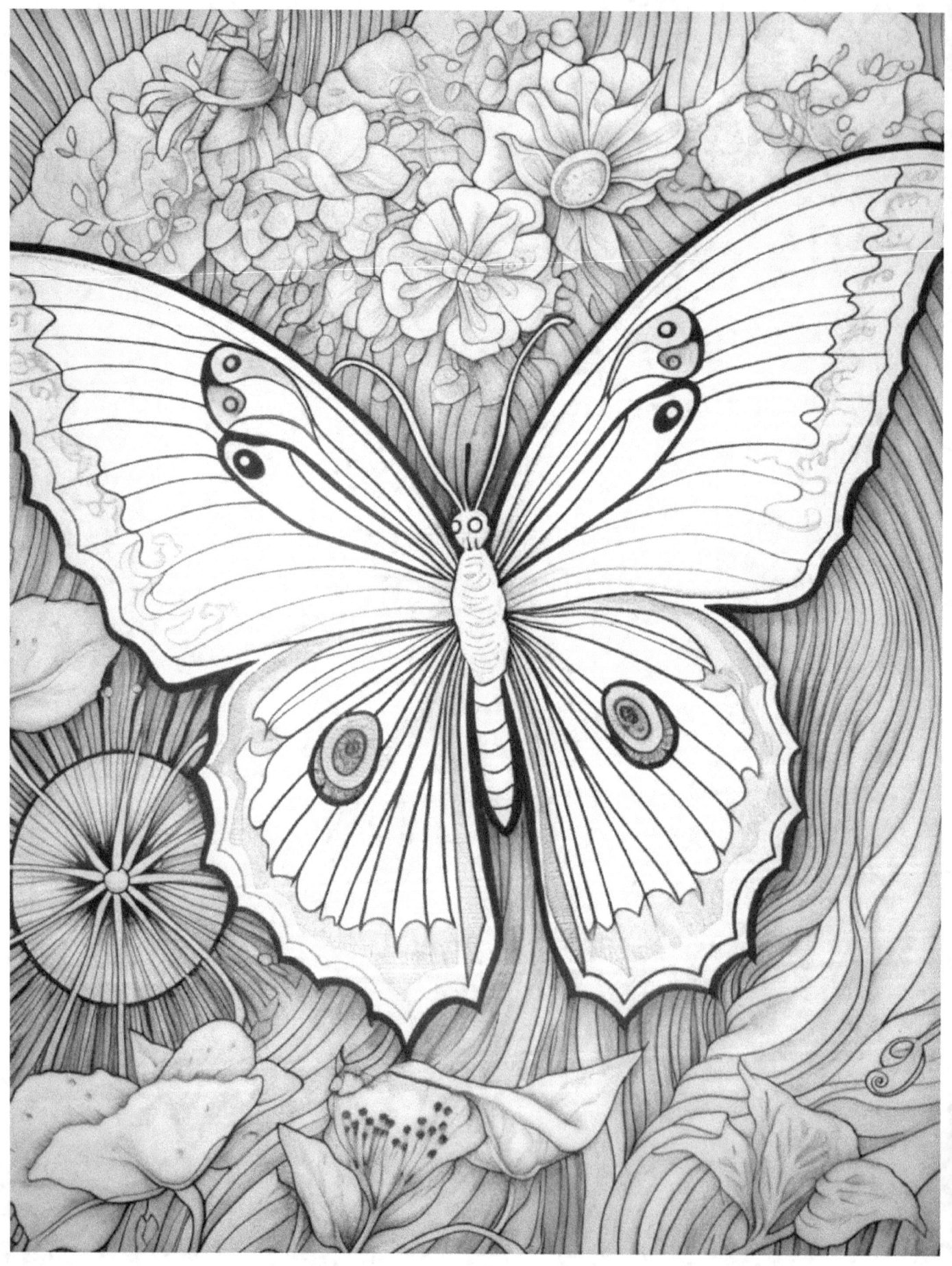

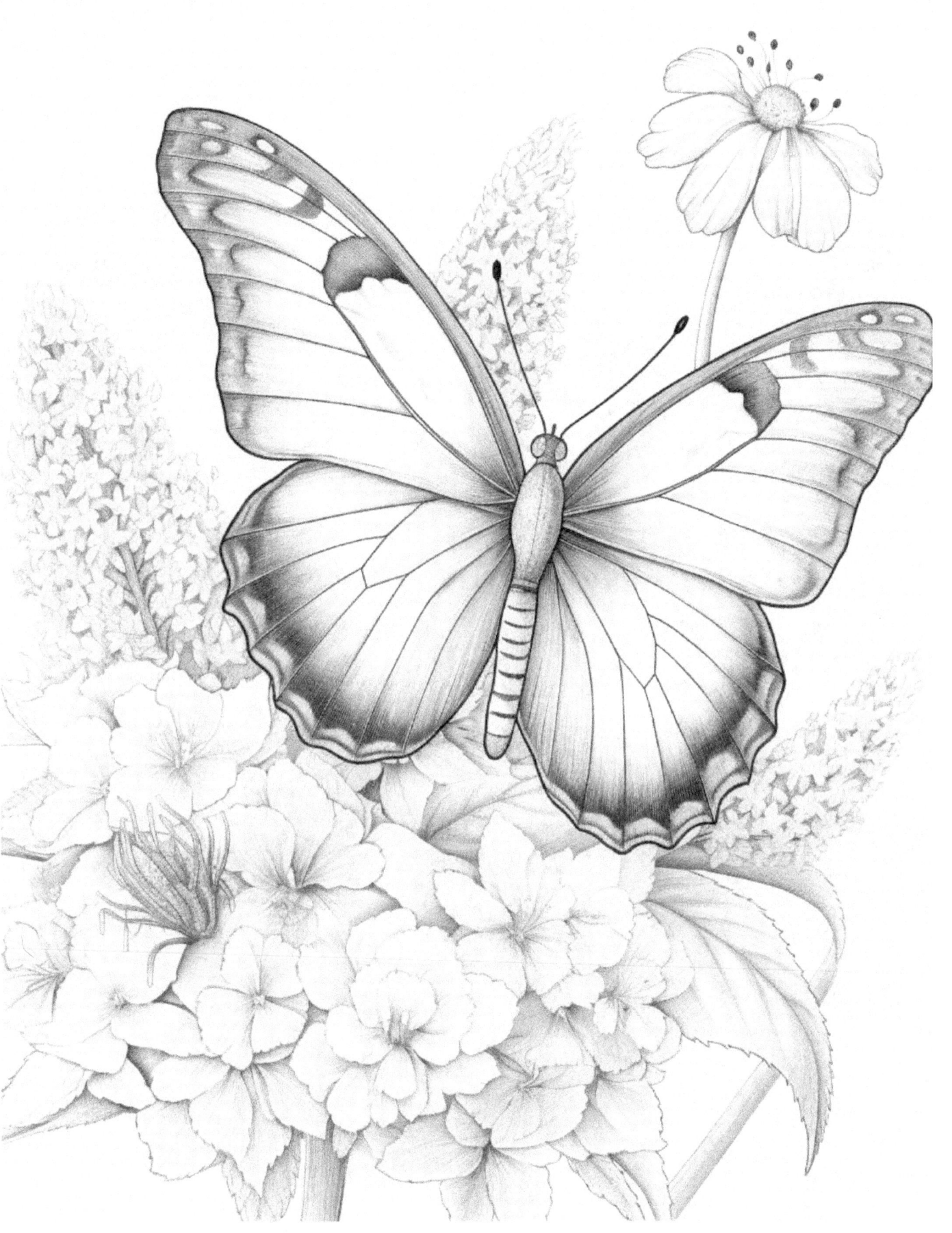

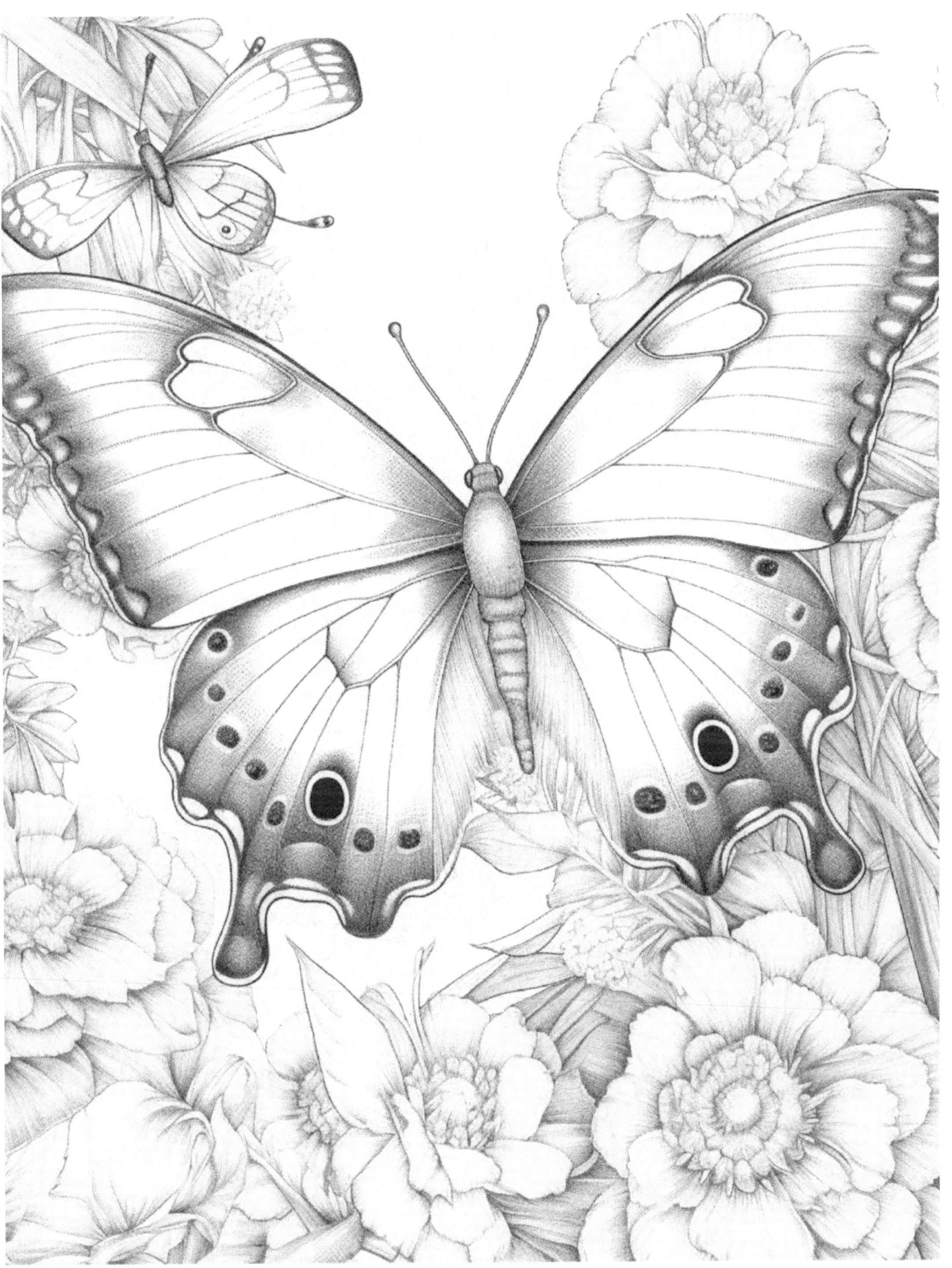

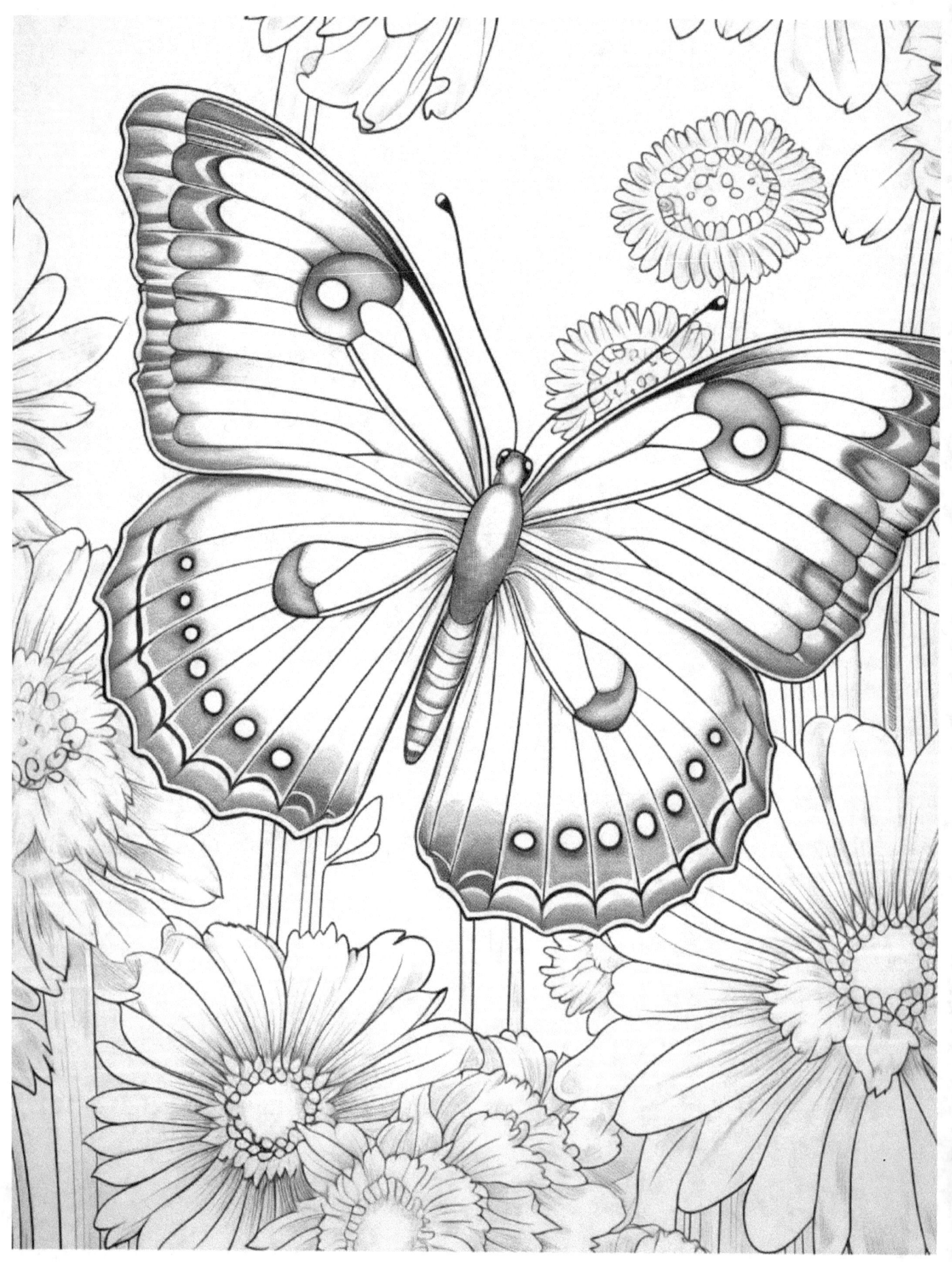

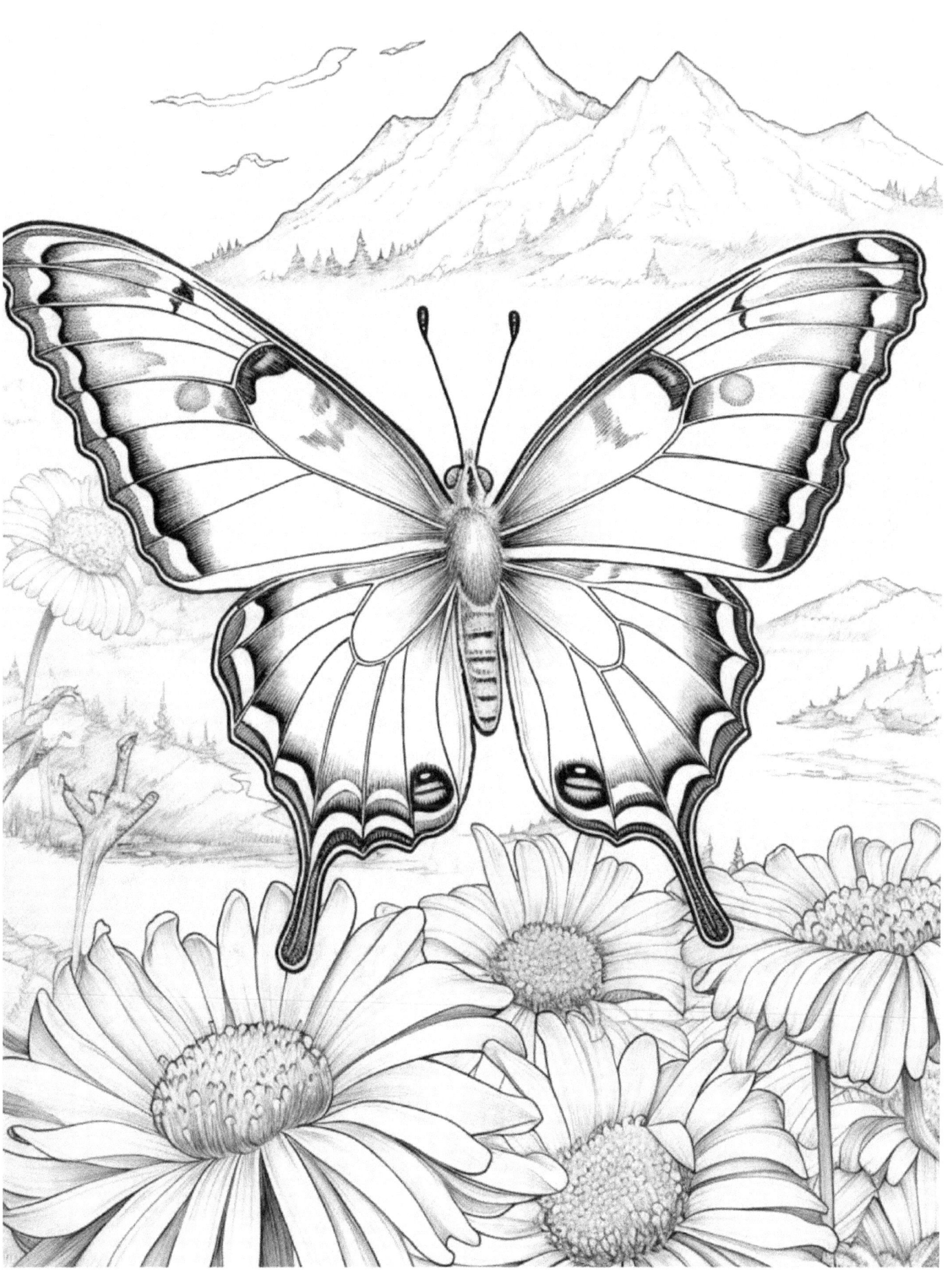

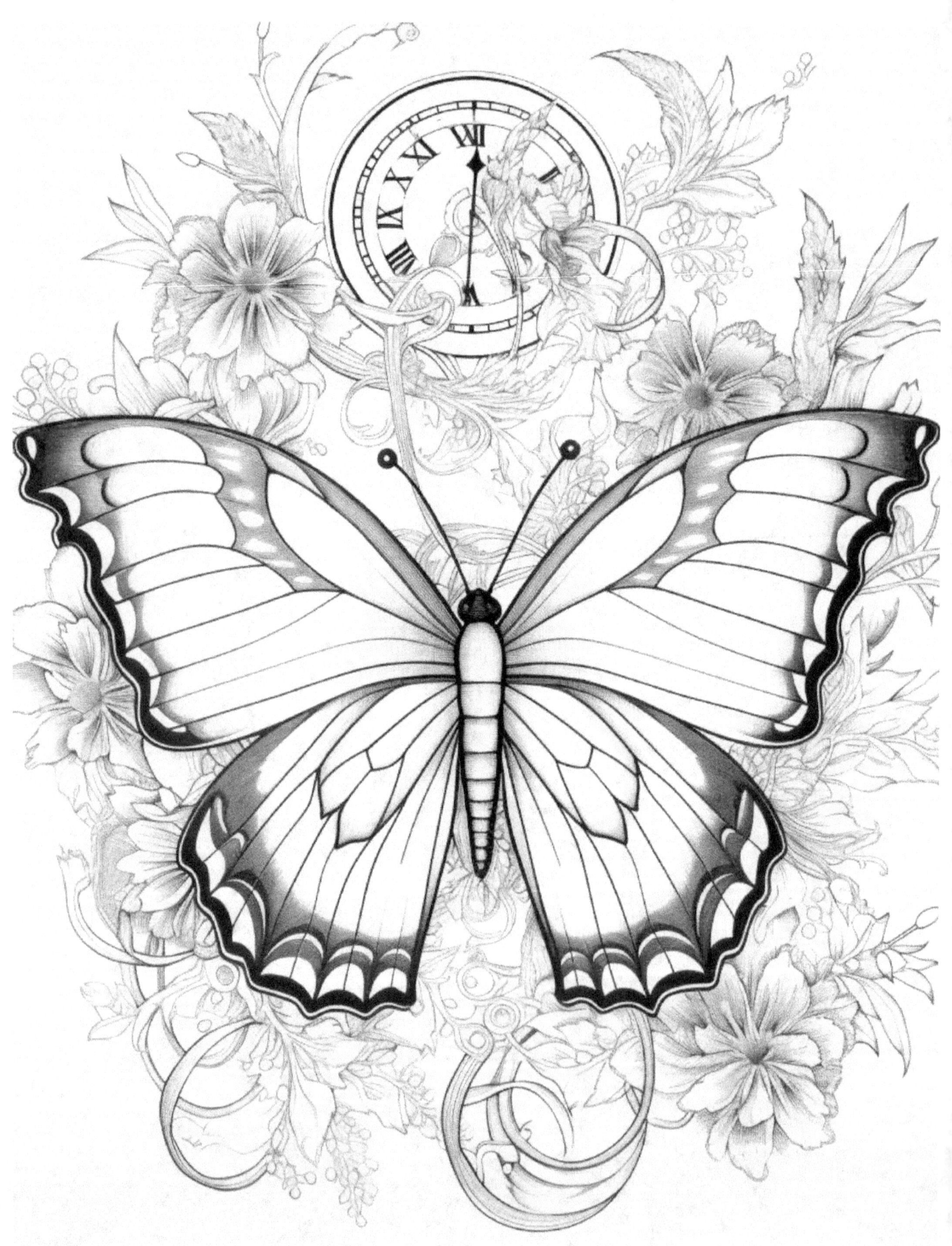

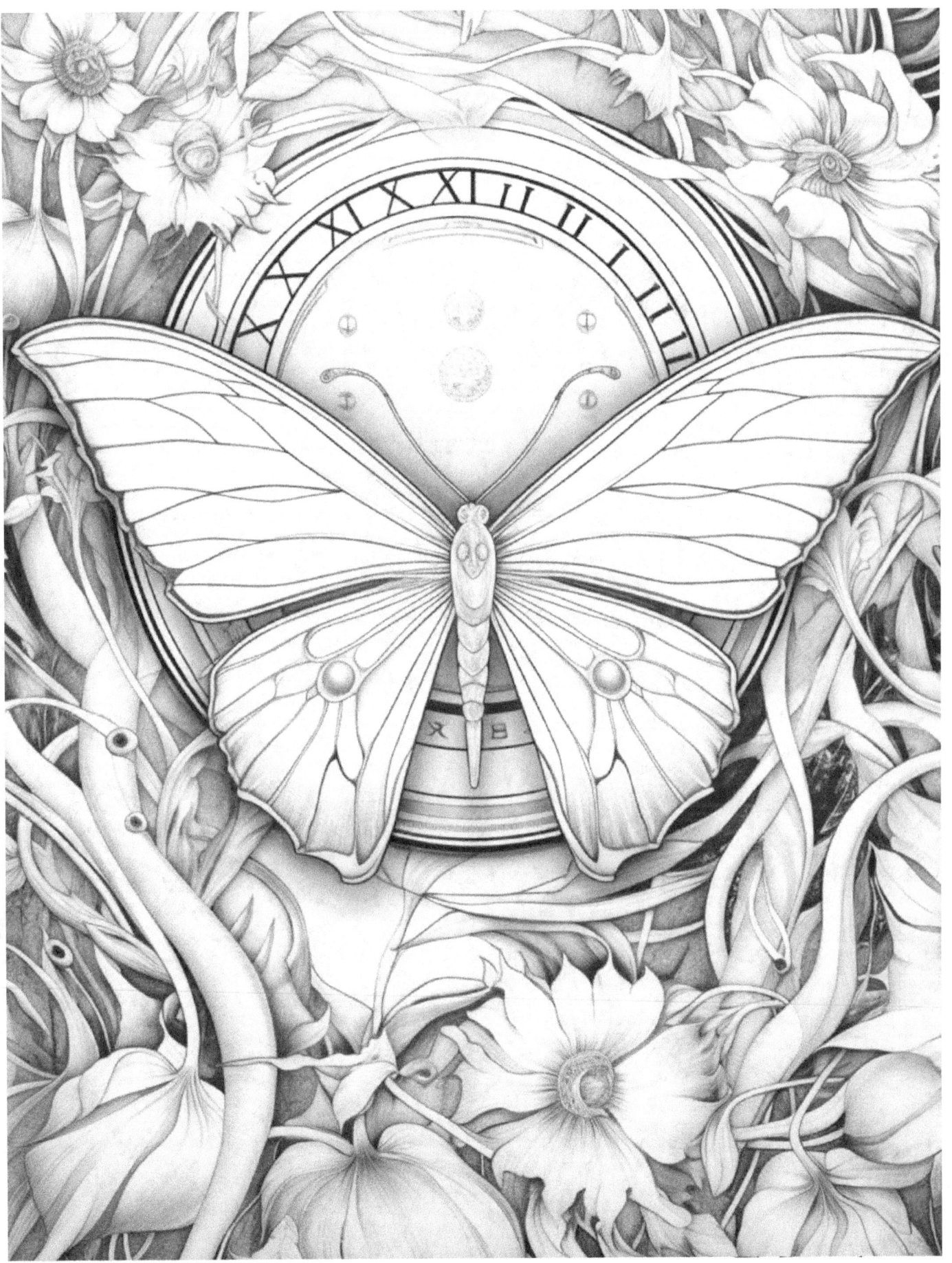

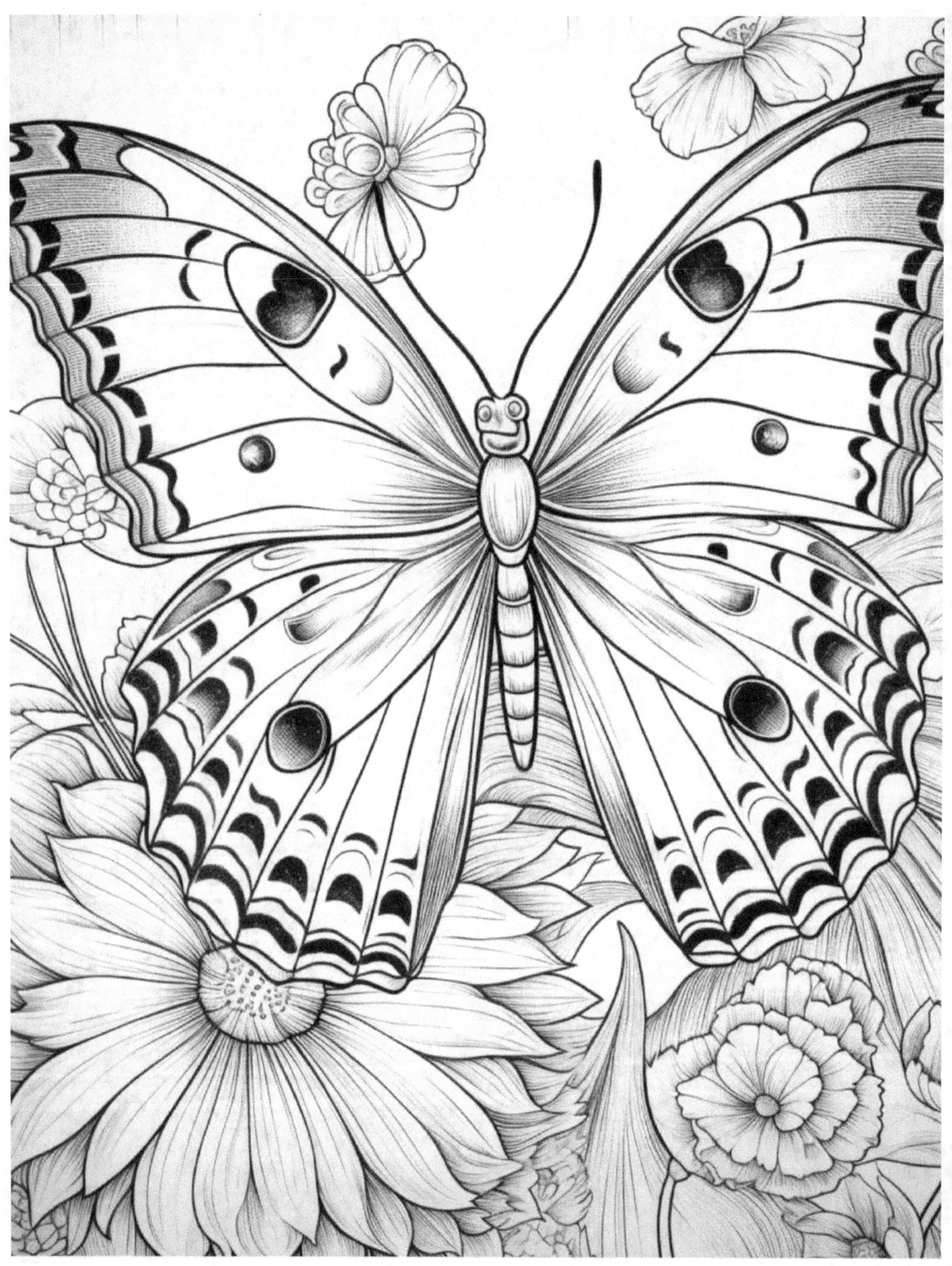

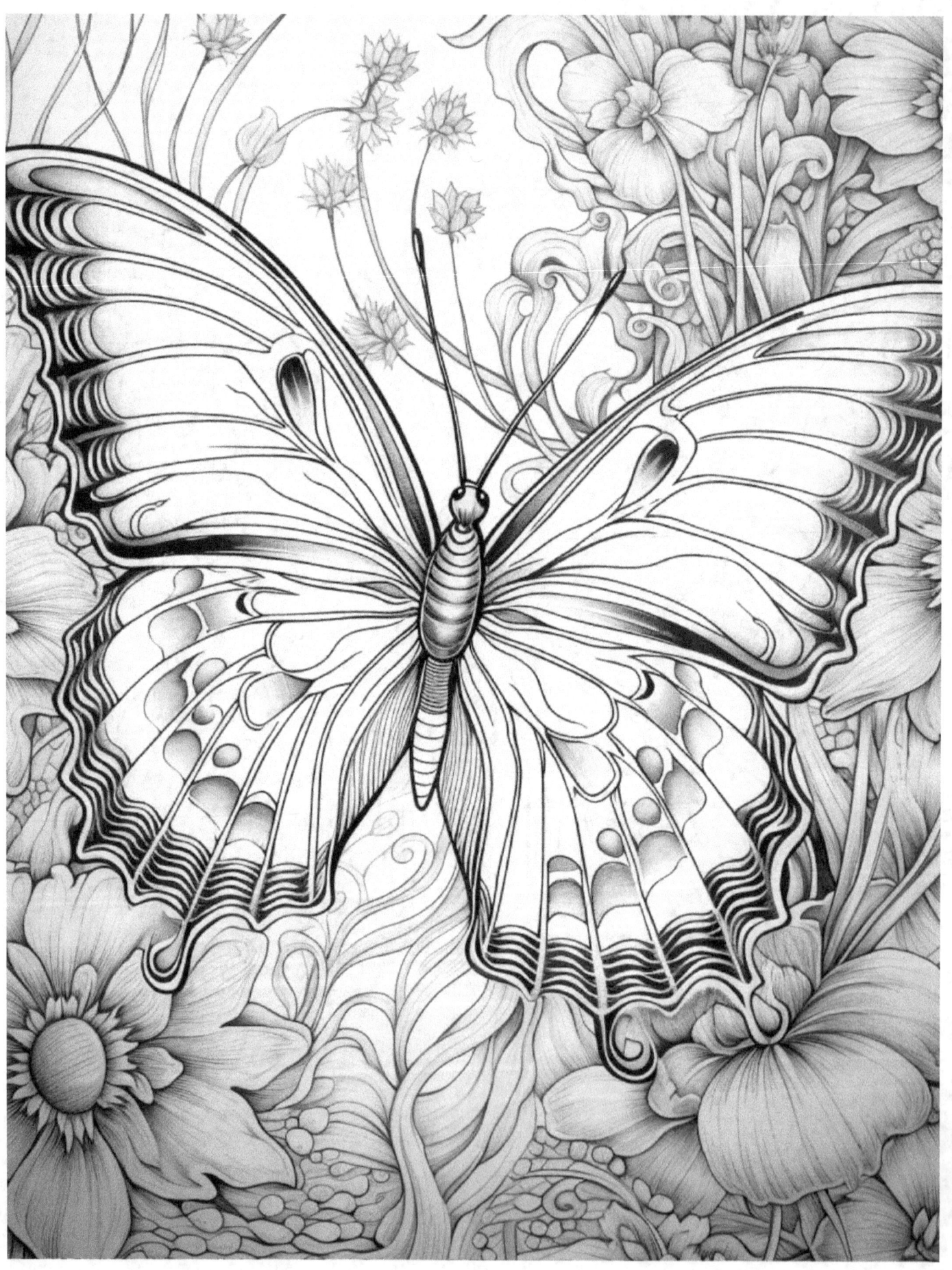

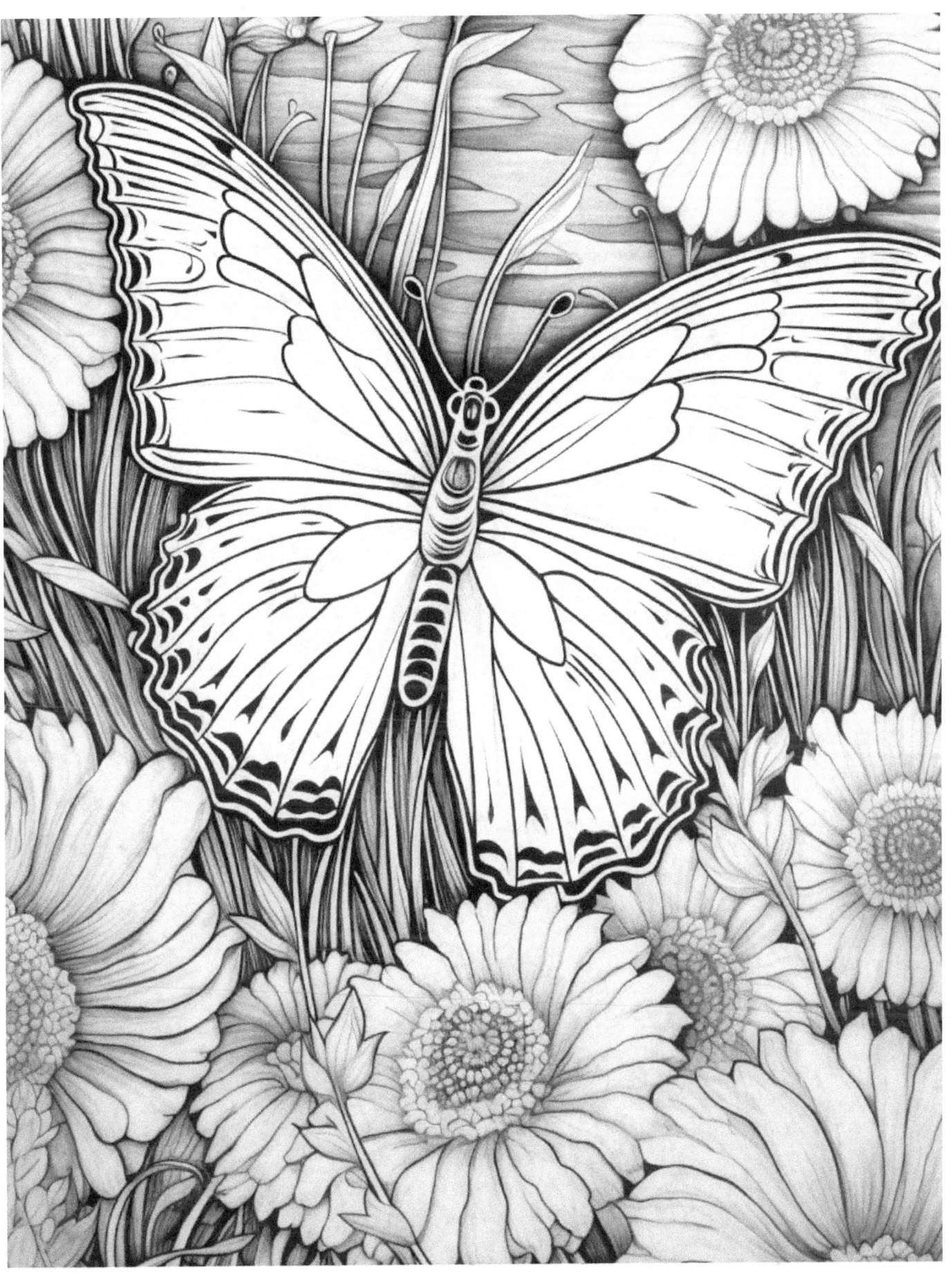

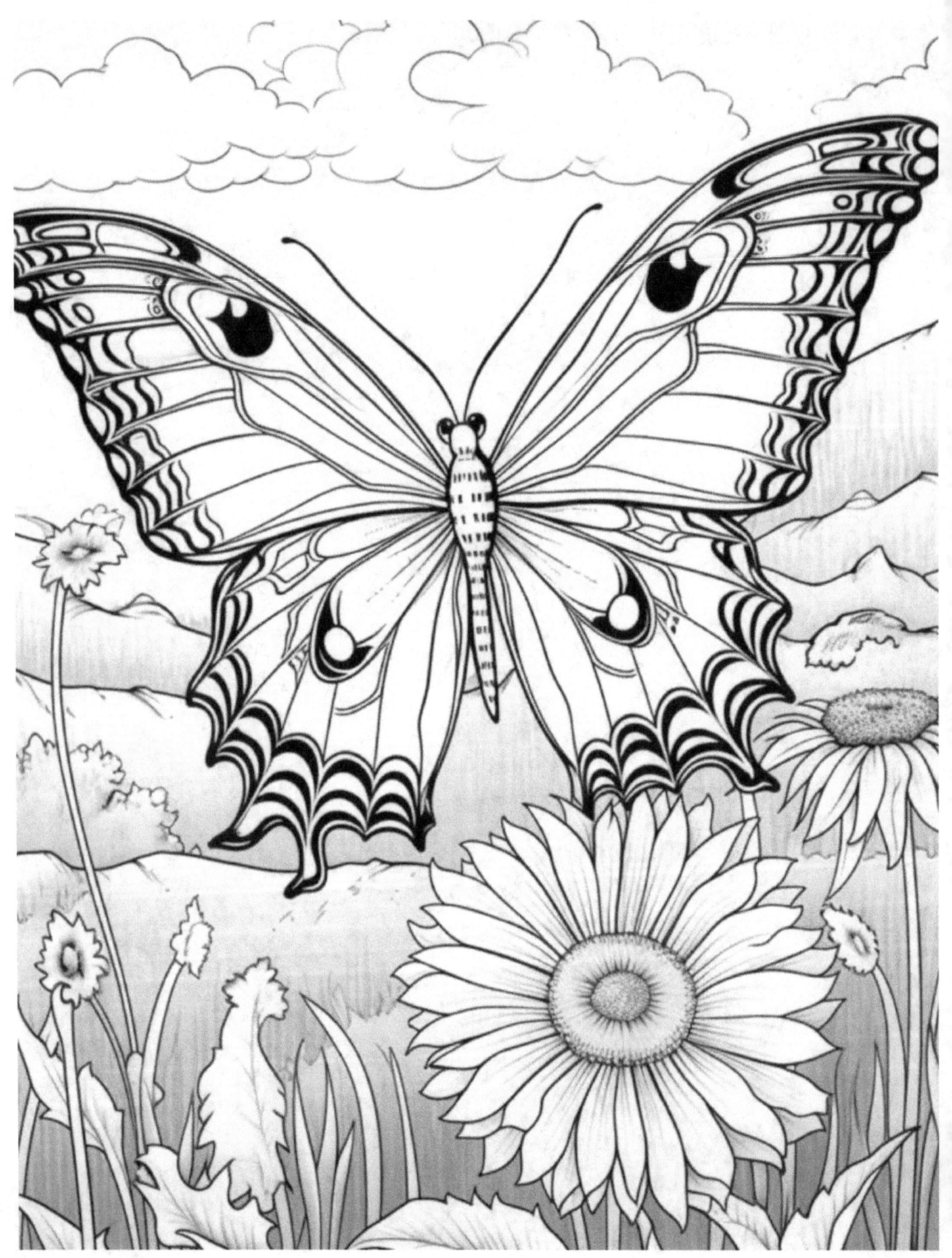

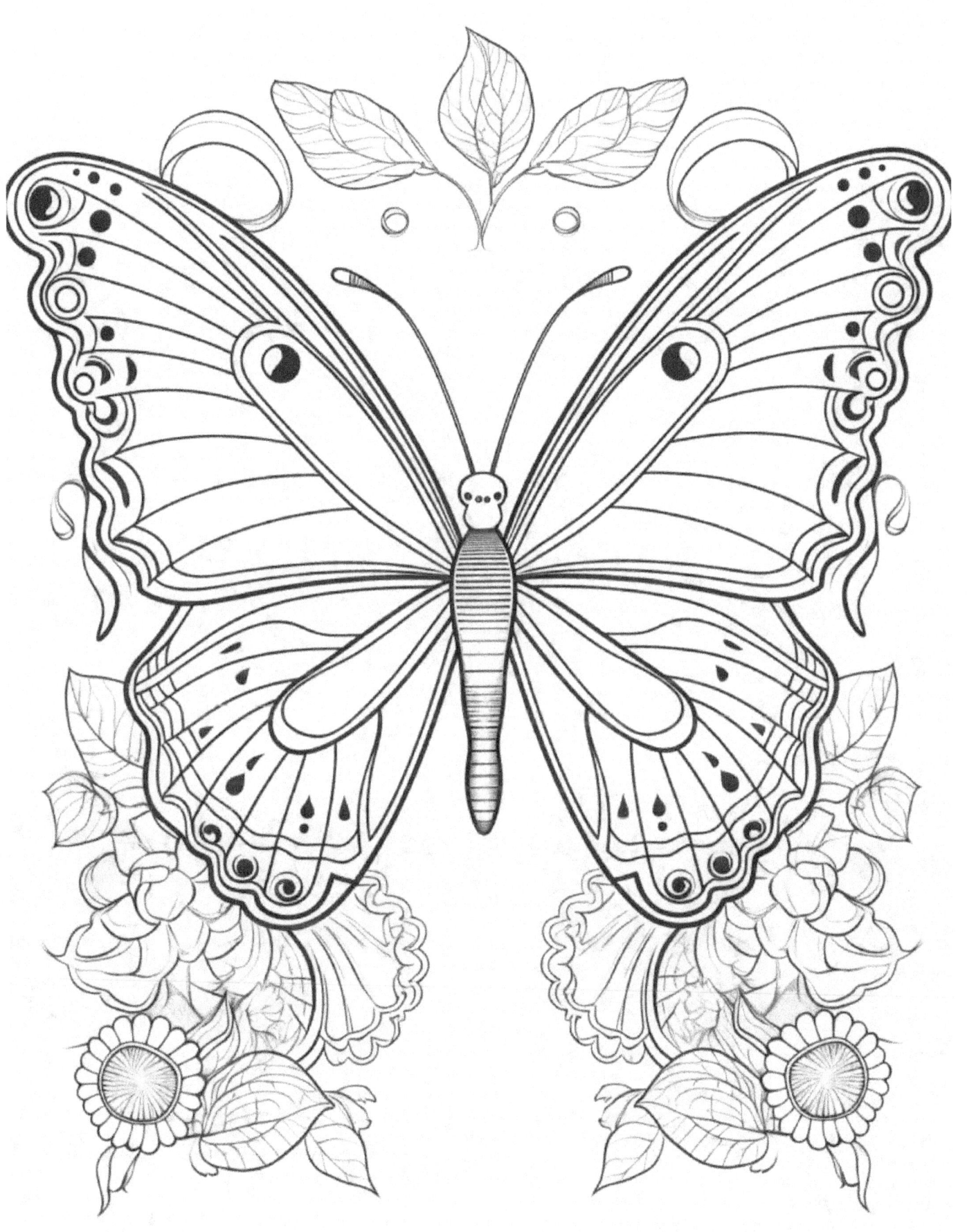

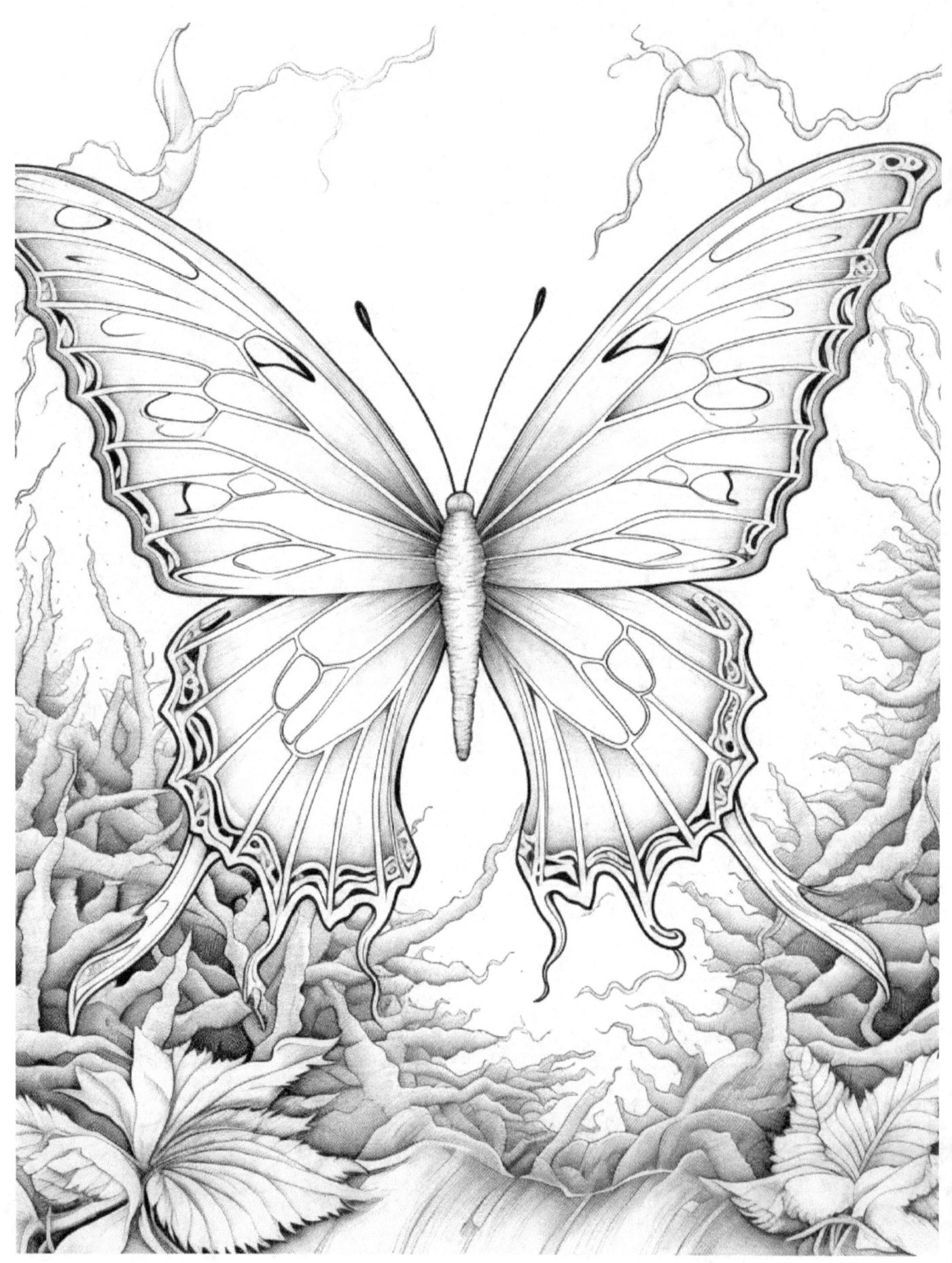

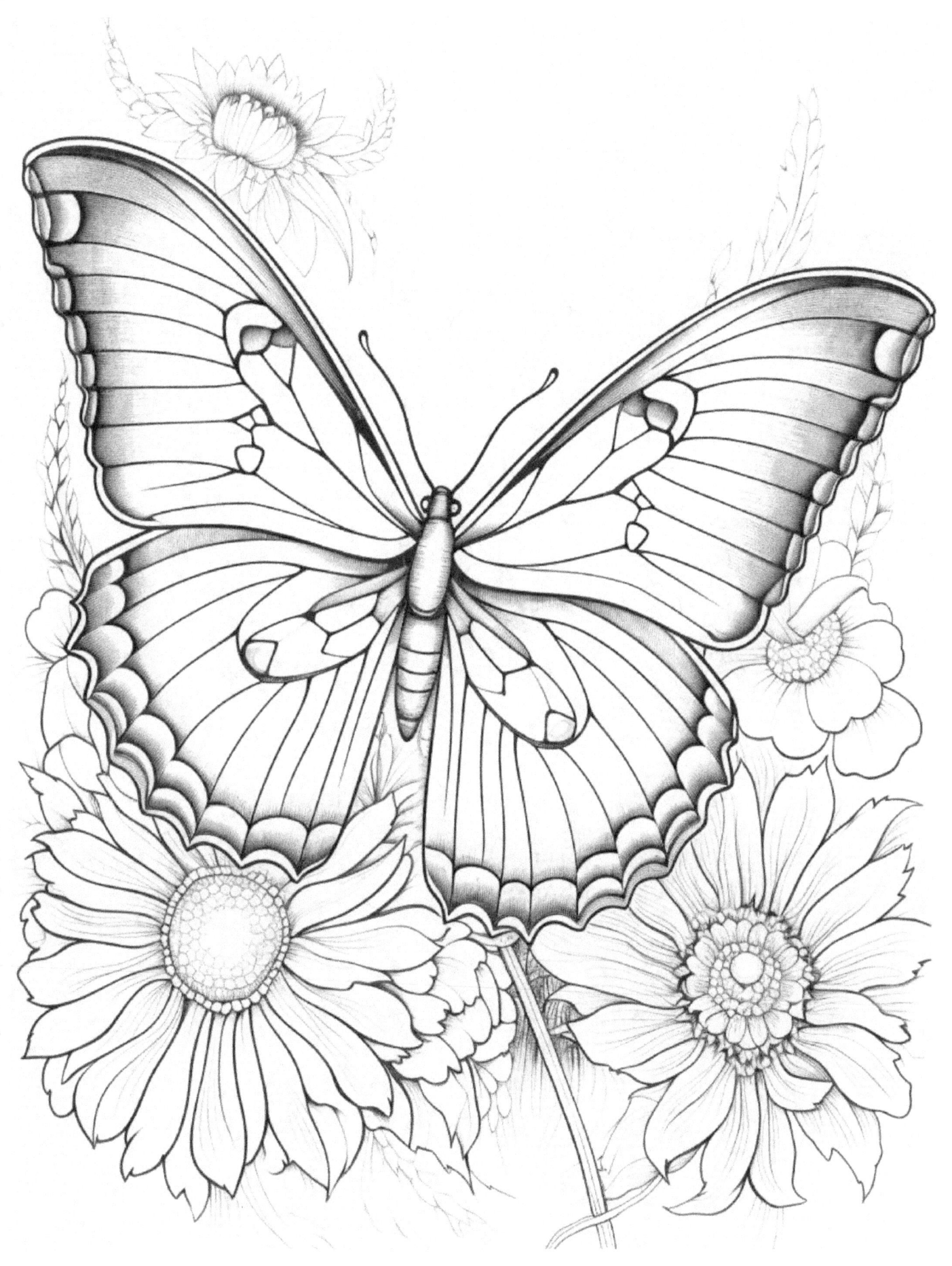

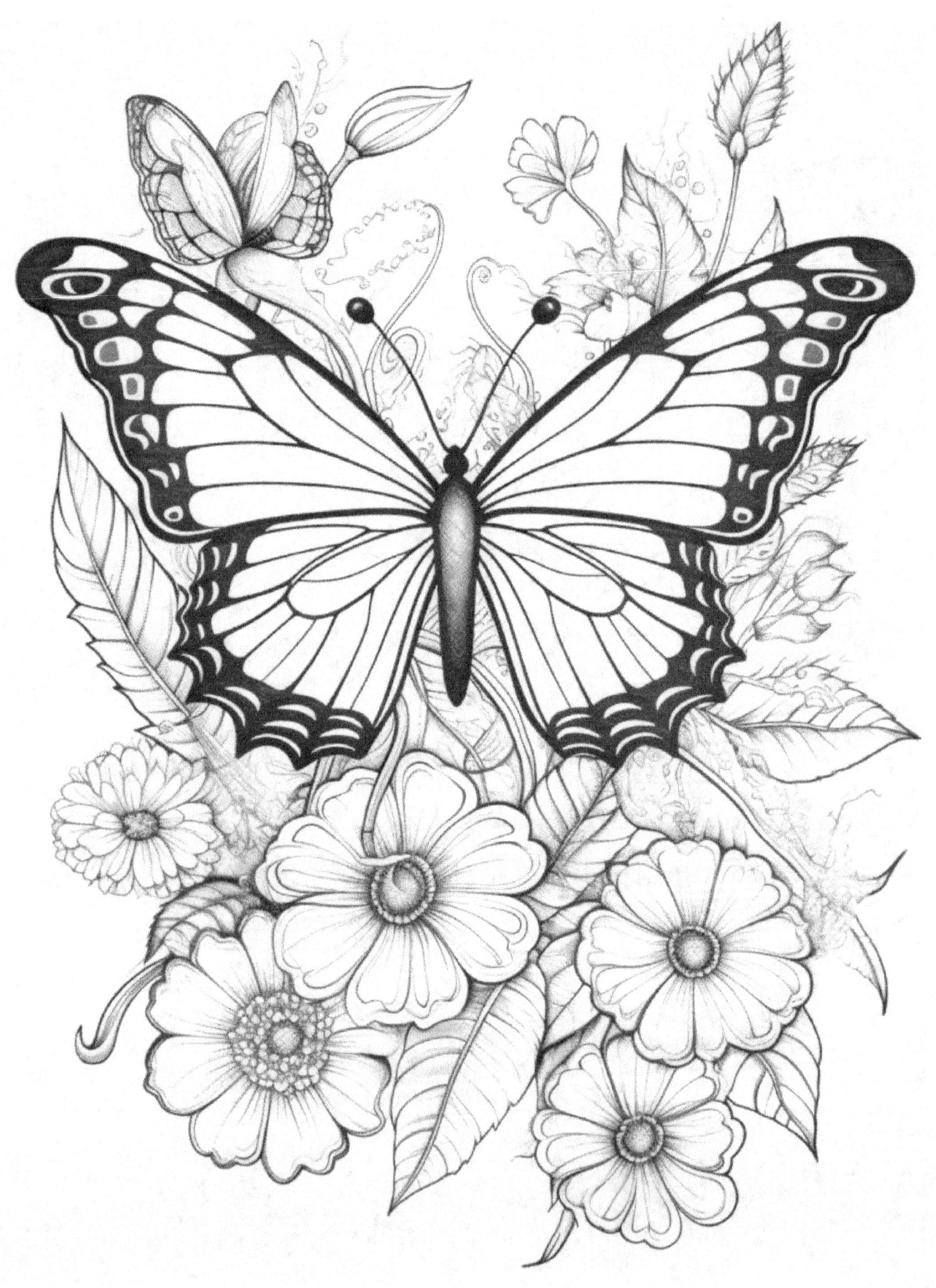

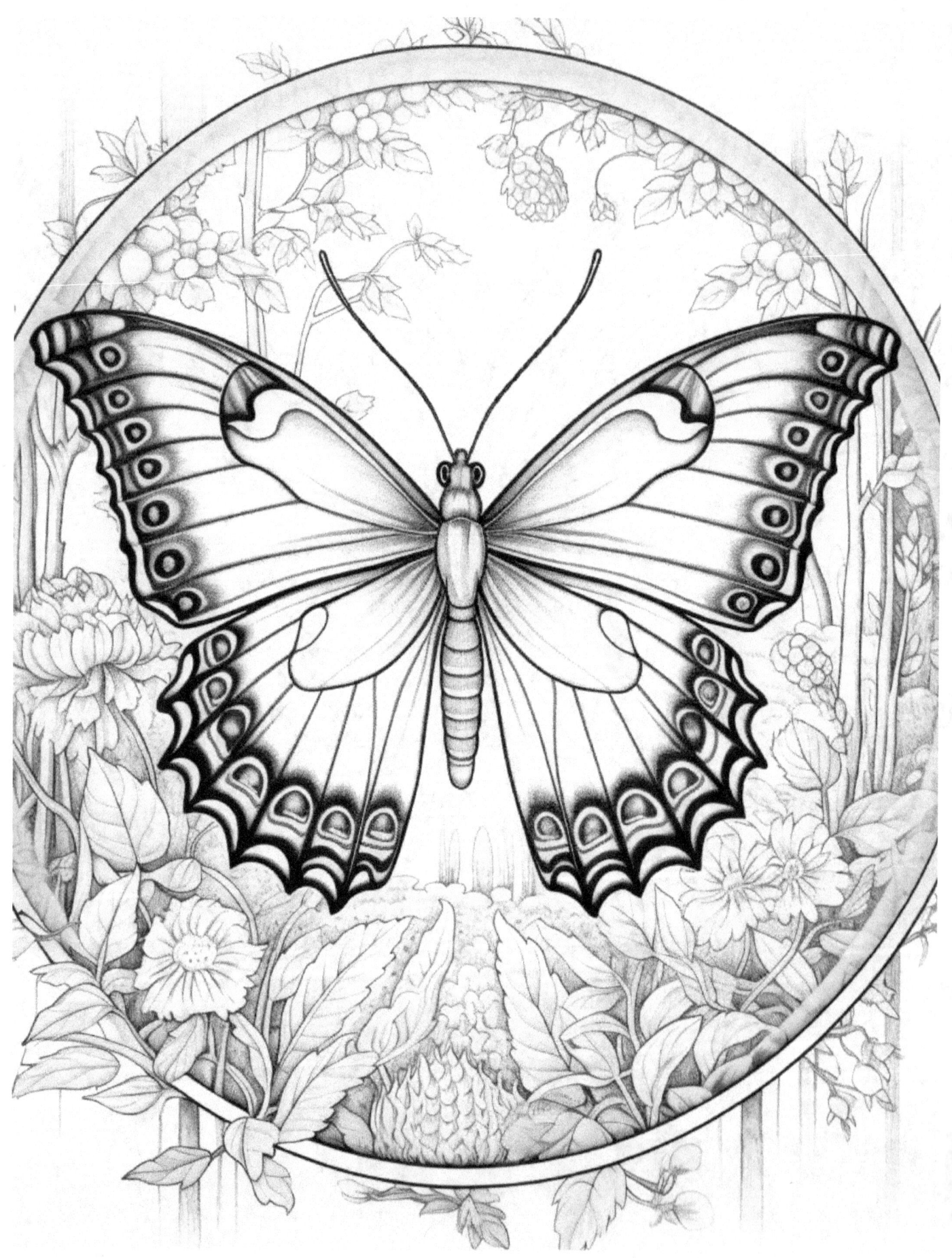

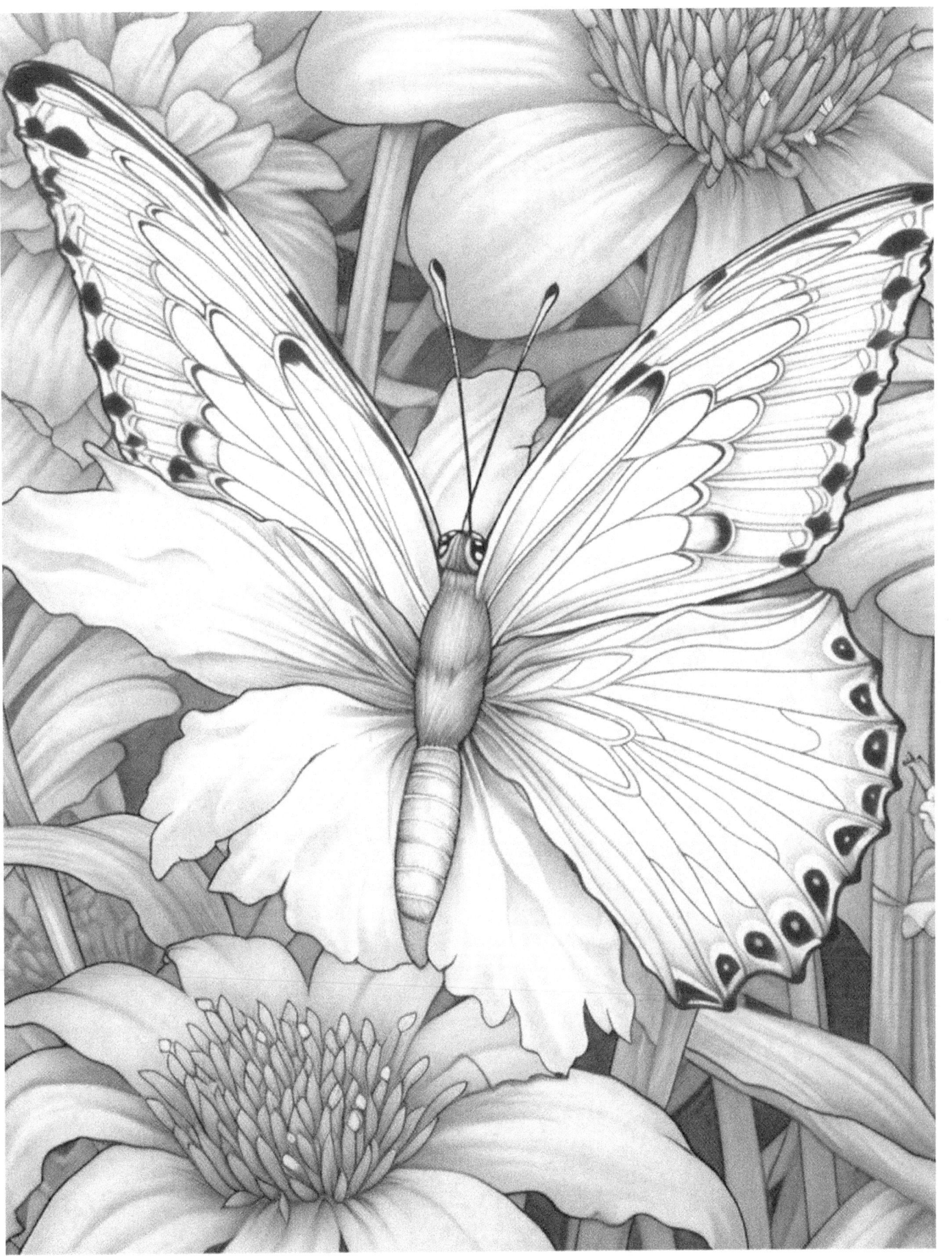

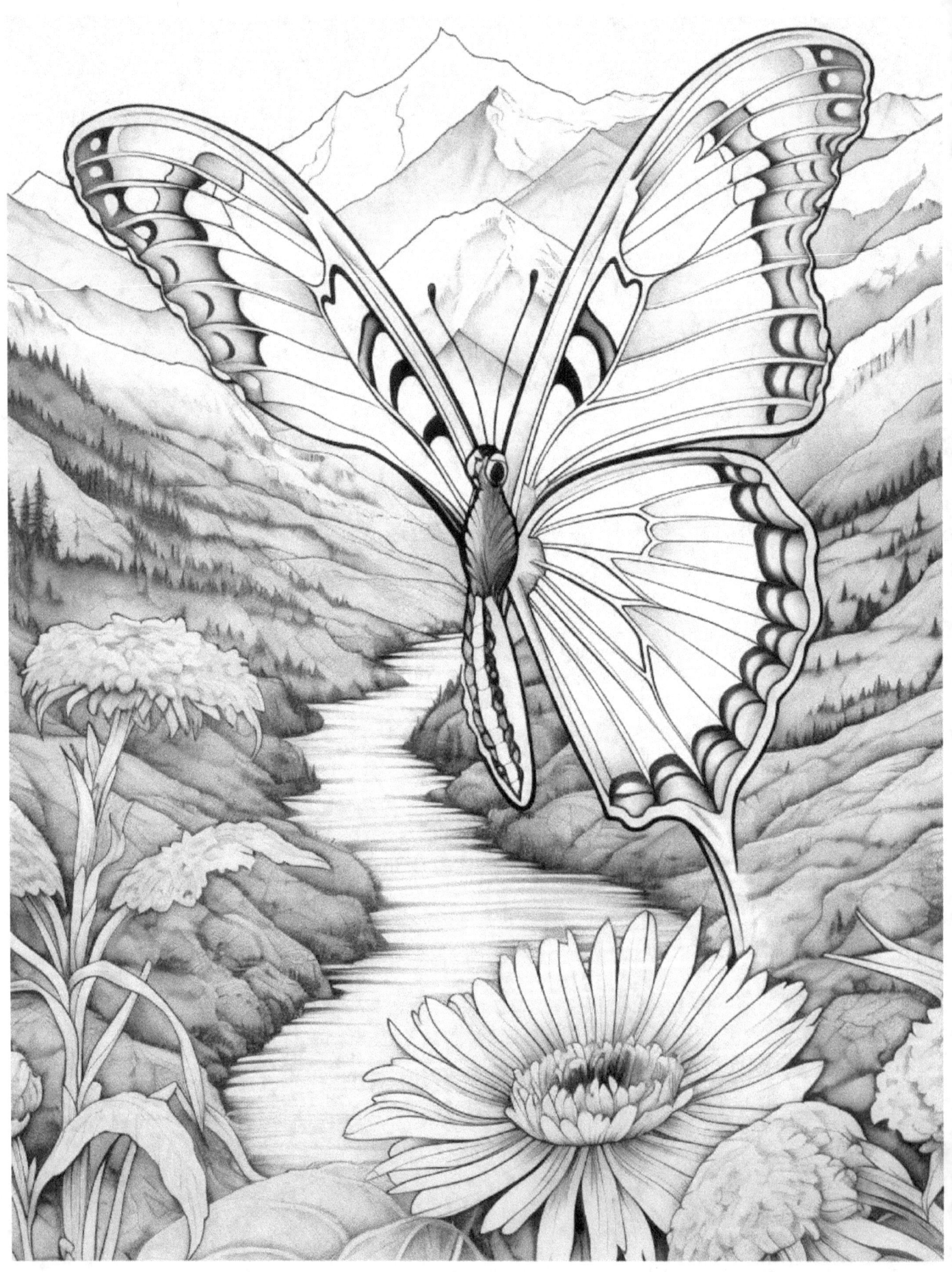

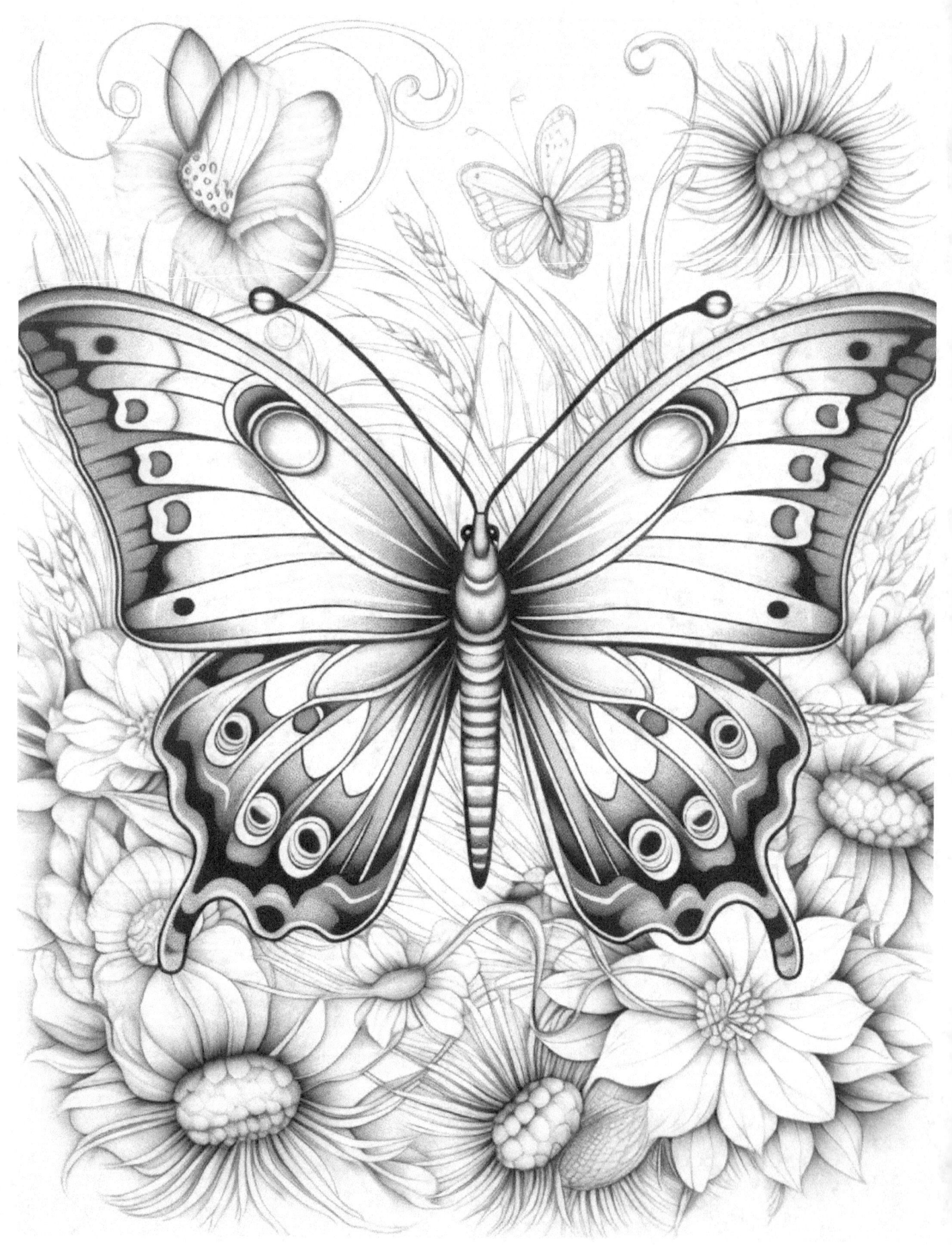

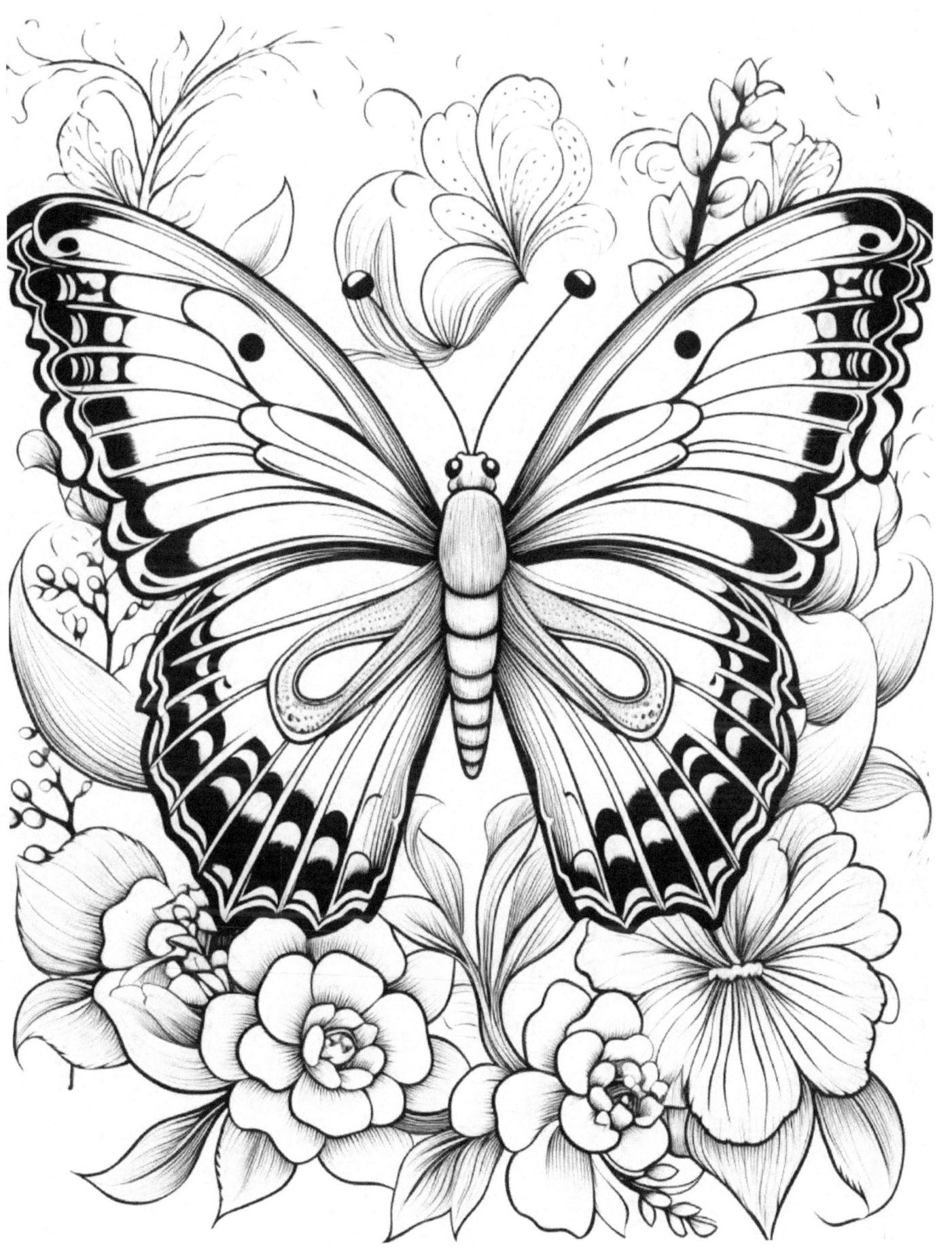

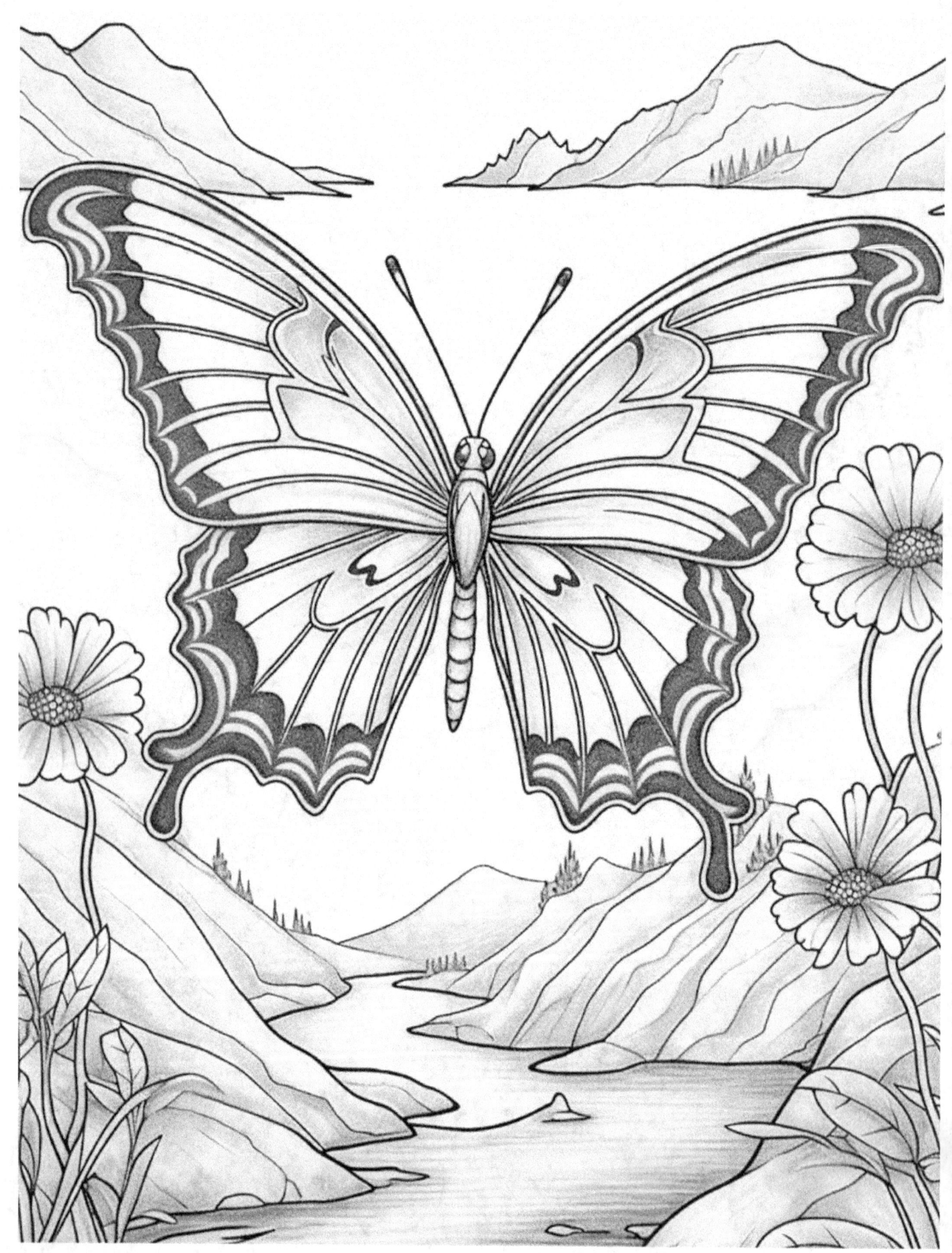

www.ingramcontent.com/pod-product-compliance
Lightning Source LLC
Chambersburg PA
CBHW082205220526
45470CB00010B/3050

9 798326 069467